20 STEPS
TO
BETTER WRITING

20 STEPS
TO
BETTER WRITING

Harry Shaw

1980

LITTLEFIELD, ADAMS & CO.
Totowa, New Jersey

Reprinted 1976, 1978, 1980

Library of Congress Cataloging in Publication Data
Shaw, Harry   20 Steps to Better Writing
(A Littlefield, Adams Quality Paperback No. 289)   1.   English language—Rhetoric.   I.   Title. PE1408.S4746   808'.042   75-1499 ISBN 0-8226-0289-X

Printed in the United States of America

Contents

v

To the Reader

The book you hold in your hands is unlike other books on the subject of becoming a writer. It is not a "grammar book." It is not a rhetoric. It is not a handbook of rules and regulations. It is not a set of theories about the ultimate aims of art. It is not a discussion of the great themes of literature.

Instead, it offers practical comment on the attitudes with which everyone should approach writing. It tries to remove some of the false notions about writing that have been developed and expanded in recent years. Above all, it seeks to single out, define, and explain the essential steps—and only the essential steps—that everyone must take in attempts to make writing not only literate but competent.

It should be noted, however, that "steps" is a word more convenient than accurate. One normally thinks of "a step" as movement or pattern. One "steps" forward or backward, up or down, to one side or the other. Also, everyone "takes steps" one at a time in a specific pattern.

As used in the title of this book and developed throughout its length, *step* means "activity," "suggestion," "process," "approach," "guideline," or "tip." It has a meaning of "beginning to act," of "setting about putting something into operation." No one should assume that "taking" any step in this book is as precise and limited an action as moving one foot and leg past another. Nor can most of the so-called steps in this book be "taken" in exact order, one, two, three, and so on.

A major difficulty with writing is that one is supposed to

"know everything" before he gets a real chance to study and practice writing. Steps in writing not only overlap; they coalesce into one giant step.

Despite this problem and despite the acknowledged inexactness of its title, this book begins with four steps that everyone should take before he begins actually to write. And it concludes with five steps—really five tests—that should be rigorously applied to every "finished" piece of writing.

These nine chapters, and the eleven intervening ones, are based upon the more than three decades of work that I have had as a teacher, writer, editor, and publisher. What they contain is my distilled experience as an author and my close observation of thousands of students of writing, ranging from those of senior high school and college age to professional writers of full-length books, novels, short stories, articles, essays, and poems. The book does not discuss everything that could be said about the involved process of becoming a better writer, but it does pinpoint what I consider those basics, those essentials, without which writing is a wasteful, time-consuming, self-defeating, and frustrating enterprise.

Yes, learning to write better requires effort—hard, dedicated, unremitting, thoughtful work. But writing can be a highly rewarding activity. The late H. L. Mencken once said "There is in writing the constant joy of sudden discovery, of happy accident." Hopefully, this modest book may help you to a "sudden discovery" of yourself and to the "happy accident" of bringing off writing that is more polished, more meaningful, more communicative than anything you have ever done before.

H. S.

20 STEPS
TO
BETTER WRITING

Understand What Writing Is

Everyone who doesn't write regularly or professionally is likely to have several incorrect notions about writing and what it involves.

Such misconceptions are understandable: most people have had little experience with actual writing. Personal and business letters, a job application or two, answers on school examinations, possibly a few reports at work or "research" papers for a book club or other organization constitute the slim total of isolated and fragmentary writing efforts many persons have made. It is not easy to understand a process with which we are unfamiliar.

Actually, writing is a comparatively late development in the progress of mankind from savagery to the present day. When you consider that "man" has been on the earth for several million years but has been working with an alphabet system of writing for only some five thousand years, the fact that everyone has difficulty understanding language—especially the act of writing—is hardly surprising. Remember also that man discovered how to mass produce alphabetic writing only a little over five hundred years ago. The idea that everybody should learn to read and write has been current for only two hundred years—and that idea is not universally held.

No one knows when and where speech originated, but apparently mankind has been making understandable sounds for hundreds of thousands of years. Writing is a relatively new art form, or process, or means of communication about which little is known. Consequently, it is all the more important that the opinions one does hold about writing should be accurate and helpful.

Four commonly accepted ideas about writing should be carefully examined.

1. WRITING IS A FORM OF SPEAKING

Although writing and speaking share a common goal of communication, they differ in several ways. A speech has been called "an essay walking on its hind legs," but effective speaking is quite different from the oral rendering of a written composition. Similarly, written composition has been prepared according to requirements and specifications not applying to speaking.

We are normally more relaxed in talking than writing, less worried about rules and errors. This is as it should be, but what many people might consider acceptable in speech they would frown upon if it appeared in writing. Some words and expressions used in writing would seem pretentious and stuffy if they appeared in speech.

Good writing is expected to be somewhat different, on occasion, from informal speech and conversation. This is a normal, justified expectation. No matter what some dictionary-makers and linguists heatedly maintain, an attitude of "anything goes" can be, and repeatedly is, costly in business and social affairs. The late Will Rogers was genuinely humorous when he remarked "A lot of people who don't say *ain't*, *ain't* eatin'." True, and yet in certain situations, using *ain't*, misspelling a word, employing an unidiomatic expression, or saying *went* when *gone* is indicated can cost a job, advancement, a social opportunity, or even a potential friend. Learning to write good English has many values, one of which is practicality.

In speaking, one's sentences are shorter—or should be—than many he might construct in writing. Language is usually more direct and much simpler in speech than in writing. Conversations that sound "all right" often seem thin, shallow, and even stupid when reduced to writing. For most people, talking is habitual, natural, informal, and relaxed. Writing is none of these.

Someone reading what you have written is usually alone or in a room free from distractions. Someone listening to you is more often surrounded by others and is sometimes distracted by them. Even when a listener is at home, following talk over TV or radio, his mind tends to wander and he cannot recapture what he has missed by rereading something written. Most people are more eye-minded than ear-minded. Something written can be read and reread many times. A spoken message has only one hearing.

Being able to speak well is no guarantee that one can write well. Many effective talkers are poor writers; few accomplished writers are good speakers. Writing and speaking are different forms of language.

2. WRITING SHOULD BE AS EASY AND SIMPLE AS SPEAKING

Perhaps if we had been writing as long and as much as we have been speaking, writing would be easier and simpler. But everyone learns to write several years after he learns to make sounds. Further, it is true that most people speak more words in a month than they write in a lifetime. A normal speaking rate is one hundred words a minute. If you talk for two hours a day—some persons talk more than this, some less—you would utter 12,000 words in a day. In a week at this rate, you would speak the length of a novel of 84,000 words. In a month, you would deliver yourself of 360,000 words; in a year more than four million. In his busy, productive lifetime, not even Shakespeare wrote that much.

What is remarkable is not that our writing is bad but that it is as good as it is, considering the effort and time spent on it.

3. WRITING REQUIRES INSPIRATION

Regardless of training or experience, everyone finds writing so difficult that he often wishes some stimulus, some insight, some flash of understanding would come to his aid. Even so accomplished a writer as Voltaire, one of the world's all-time literary masters, wrote: "The necessity of writing something, the embarrassment produced by the consciousness of having nothing to say, and the desire to exhibit ability are three things sufficient to render even a great man ridiculous."

Actually, success in writing depends upon constant, unremitting, earnest application and not upon so-called "flashes of inspiration" and sudden bursts of effort. Two wise and often-quoted remarks of Thomas A. Edison are these: "There is no substitute for hard work" and "Genius is one percent inspiration and ninety-nine percent perspiration."

Robert Littell, a professional writer and editor, once wrote: "Inspiration? A question that is sure to be raised. It's not a visitation, of course, but is inside you all the time. Don't wait for it; keep on writing and writing and ever so often it will come roaring up out of your insides and take the pencil from your hands. Nobody knows how to coax it up. Don't press, as the golfers say. . . . The shy beast will come up or not, as he chooses."

The consensus of experienced writers is that the only way to woo inspiration is to apply the seat of the pants to the seat of a chair hour after hour and day after day, constantly writing and rewriting.

4. WRITING IS A COMPLICATED SERIES OF *DO'S* AND *DON'T'S*

A major reason for the tightening up, or partial paralysis, of people starting to write is their attitude. They look upon writing as "a bunch of grammar," a long, intricate string of *thou-shalt-not's*. Actually, nearly everyone who can communicate by speaking knows quite enough "grammar" to write effectively. English grammar is only "the English way of saying things." What is bothersome is not grammar but *usage*, a problem treated in many of the remaining "steps" in this book.

You do not need to know the principle of the combustion engine in order to drive an automobile. But you do need to know where to insert the ignition key, how to start the motor, how to work an automatic or manual shift, steer, follow road signs, and apply brakes. Skilled drivers are so proficient in these operations that they do them "without thinking."

Neither are skilled writers (or speakers) always consciously aware of grammar. A professional writer might be unable to define an adjective, but he would "instinctively" change the phrase "a night when the wind blew" to "windy night," if he felt the former to be too long and not quite effective. You might not know what a clause and a phrase are and thus would not know how to "reduce predication." But your ear or common sense or even a little "grammar" might enable you to reduce "Diphtheria, which used to be a deadly disease, is now rare" to the shorter and more direct "Diphtheria, once a deadly disease, is now rare." Every effective writer has a working knowledge of words and their ways. And that is all that grammar is.

Try to approach writing as what it is: a flexible, resourceful medium that will help you communicate clearly and interestingly to and with others. What possible activity could be more important or more meaningful to you or to anyone?

STEP TWO

Preplan Everything You Write

Writing is not a single operation. It is a process consisting of three parts: preplanning, writing, and revising. Broken into its three phases, writing will both seem and actually be less complicated and difficult.

A finished piece of writing may be likened to the part of an iceberg that appears above water, one-ninth of the total mass. The remaining eight-ninths consists of preplanning (or prewriting) and revising.

You have been "speaking prose" constantly since you began to talk. You have also been engaged in a form of writing since first-grade days. Haven't you uttered many remarks to yourself before saying them aloud? Haven't you "thought through" many letters or memos before putting them on paper? Many a businessman fluently dictates effective letters to a secretary or machine because he put himself to sleep the night before planning what he would say. "Thinking ahead" is not often thought of as writing, but it is an important, even essential part of that process.

If you will sit down to write *what you have thought* and not sit down to think *what you will write,* the difficulties in actual writing will diminish. They will not disappear, but they will not seem so formidable and frightening. When driving along a highway, have you ever noticed that in the distance the road seemed to rise sharply up a steep hill? As you sped along, however, the incline apparently smoothed out, became less vertical. The same effect will be obtained in writing if you approach it gradually through the act of planning ahead.

No matter what kind of writing you intend to do, preplanning is important. It's true, though, that if your goal is only to write better business or personal letters or other such everyday types of communication, relatively little prewriting is necessary. In writing a business memo, or report, or a short book review, you are certain to do some thinking ahead but hardly an extensive or involved amount of actual planning.

But if your aim is to become a professional writer or to learn to write more effectively for pleasure and as a means of self-expression, then some genuine prethinking is essential. Prewriting is not merely a means of discovering something to write about. It involves willingness and desire to think your own thoughts. Time spent in prewriting is time spent in sorting out our own thoughts, in exploring why we have them, and in reaching some conclusions about their identity and why they interest us.

SELF-EVALUATION

The first common-sense approach to preplanning is self-evaluation. Most of us exist for years at a time without doing what an efficient storekeeper does periodically—take stock.

A sensible starting place is to think about what the members of your family mean and have meant to you. What friends do you have and what kinds of people are they? What did whatever schooling you have had mean to you and what does it mean now? What are your ideas about religion, politics, marriage, love, hobbies, drug culture, crime, sports, work, business, and morals?

Such self-analysis is a major step in becoming a better writer—finding out things about ourselves that we have probably never realized before. Before proceeding, answer as best you can these direct, searching, important questions:

1. What are my *social* beliefs? (Do I really like people? What kinds of people? What are the qualifications necessary to gain my friendship? Do I like men better than

women? Women better than men? Do I like children, as
a general rule, occasionally, never? Have I any real concern for underprivileged people? *Why* do I hold these
attitudes?)

2. What are my *religious* beliefs? (Do I believe in God? If
so, under what aspect—as a transcendentalist, a Baptist,
as some sort of Supreme Mind? Am I agnostic or
atheistic? *Why* do I hold these beliefs?)

3. What are my *political* beliefs? (Am I interested in national and international politics? Am I a reactionary in
politics, a conservative, a radical, an extremist? What
do I mean by these terms? *Why* do I hold these
attitudes?)

4. What are my *moral* beliefs? (Do I subscribe to, and
practice, the "Golden Rule"? Do I believe that "Honesty
is the best policy"? What do I really think of the Ten
Commandments as a guide for human conduct? Do I
know all ten? Do I believe in the single or double
standard? Do I believe in the sanctity of marriage?
Romantic love? Free love? *Why* do I hold these attitudes?)

5. What do I want to be, and to be doing, five (ten) years
from now? *Why*?

6. What do I expect to be, and to be doing, five (ten) years
from now? *Why*?

7. What, for me, is the single major problem facing the
world today? Why have I selected this from many possible choices?

8. What would constitute, for me, the greatest happiness
I can imagine? The greatest disaster? *Why*?

9. Am I an observant person, alert to what is going on
about me? Am I capable of self-analysis and criticism?
Am I open-minded—tolerant of other people and their
ideas? Am I capable of reflection and meditation? Am I
aware of my limitations?

10. How did I get to be the way I am? What were (or are)
the principal events, persons, and places that have
molded my life thus far?

What you find out in pondering these questions may disappoint, please, disgust, or excite you. But it is impossible to face them squarely without realizing something about the kind of person you are, what you might be able to write about, and how you might go about doing so.

PREWRITING AND ORIGINALITY

We always find that we have to write from our own experience, observation, curiosity, imagination, and reflection. Naturally, we get much of our material from others in discussions or conversations, in interviews or lectures, or in reading. But we must assimilate all this material and make it our own. Otherwise, what we write will be not ours but someone else's. True originality is not so much a matter of substance as of individualized treatment. The most interesting and effective subjects for writing are those about which we either have some knowledge or genuinely want to learn something. Writing is made out of the ideas and impressions which we have obtained from various sources and made a part of ourselves.

In addition to thinking about the preceding ten questions, give some attention to these items that will aid in self-analysis and provide insights into sources of originality that should come before actual writing:

Memories

Can you recall how someone, or some place, or some idea seemed to you at some earlier time in your life? What can you remember about the day you entered first grade? The first (or most memorable) Christmas you can recollect? The most cruel (or kindest) thing anyone ever did to you? Your first date? The day Martin Luther King, Jr. was shot?

People and Places

Who is the most entertaining (or dullest or most arrogant) person you have ever known? What one person did you most admire when you were ten years old? Whom do you most admire today? What is the most beautiful (or appealing or restful) place you have ever seen? What is, or once seemed, the most shocking sight in your town?

Incidents and Events

What was the most appalling accident you have ever witnessed? What event in your life provided the greatest excitement? Sense of achievement? Biggest disappointment? Worst embarrassment? Of all the incidents in your life, which one do you remember with the greatest pleasure? The most shame? If you could relive one day (or one hour) in your life, what would that day (or hour) be?

Imagination and Daydreaming

If you could be any person in the world for a day (or month) whom would you choose to be? With what one person who has ever lived would you most like to have an imaginary conversation? If you had free choice and unlimited resources, in what city or century would you most like to spend a week or a year? What is your idea of a perfect day?

None of these topics and questions is guaranteed to produce workable ideas, but your mind probably will be triggered by a few of them. What remains to be done is testing this idea to see if it is usable *and* getting hold of material for its development. These necessary steps are a part of preplanning.

NEVER STOP PREWRITING

Someone has referred to preplanning as "writing on the hoof." By this is meant "writing" all the time as we go about daily activities. All authors apparently rub ideas together while walking around, eating, taking a bath, conversing, working, reading, and even sleeping. Their practice should be followed by every aspiring writer. The late Somerset Maugham, an acclaimed and successful writer, had this to say:

> The author does not only write when he's at his desk, he writes all day long, when he is thinking, when he is reading, when he is experiencing: everything he sees and feels is

significant to his purpose and, consciously or unconsciously, he is forever storing and making over his impressions.

Maugham's advice and experience are echoed by the late James Thurber:

> I never quite know when I'm not writing. Sometimes my wife comes up to me at a party and says "Stop writing." She usually catches me in the middle of a paragraph. Or my daughter will ask at the dinner table, "Is he sick?" "No," my wife replies, "he's writing."

Georges Simenon, the French novelist and mystery story writer, is quoted as saying: "I always have two or three themes in my mind. They are things about which I worry. Before I start writing, I consciously take up one of those ideas."

Robert Penn Warren, the American novelist, was once asked "What is your period of incubation?" He replied:

> Something I read or see stays in my head for five or six years. I read a short article [about the basic story of *World Enough and Time*] in five minutes. But I was six years making the novel. Any book I write starts with a flash but takes a long time to shape up. All of my first versions are in my head, so that when I sit down to write, I have some line developed in my head.

The acts of prewriting and writing overlap, but you are urged never to begin to write until you have incubated what you plan to say and how you plan to say that something, whatever it is. Time spent in preplanning will save time in writing. It will also help to make the finished product more effective.

STEP THREE

Have a Purpose in Everything You Write

When you write about something which really means something to you, something which is or was really important, your writing is interesting, even though you think it may sound flat to others. If you have a genuine purpose when you write, you need never fear that your work will lack interest. As a matter of fact, *purpose* is a second practical approach to this problem of writing. After you have made a preliminary study of yourself—that is, your experiences, observations, and ideas—you then have to consider to what purpose you are going to write about them. Writing of all kinds should have as a central purpose the communication of specific, predetermined ideas or feelings. Writing that doesn't clearly convey such feelings and ideas from you to your readers isn't really writing at all.

The dominant idea, or controlling purpose, of a letter you write to a department store or mail-order house is clear: you are protesting a charge, asking for an adjustment, returning merchandise, or whatever. You *know* in advance what you hope or expect the letter to accomplish. Without this clear purpose, the letter would be useless. Similarly, a memo or office report or a sales prospectus or job application either has a controlling purpose or is thrown in the wastebasket. What applies to these kinds of writing applies to everything that can be written: book report, speech, article, essay, poem, short story, or even novel.

Nor is it enough to say that your purpose in writing is to achieve publication, win fame, impress others, or make money.

Such so-called "purposes" are aims, hopes, and ambitions, not controlling ideas.

Purpose may be defined as the overall design that controls what you are going to try to write. This design, this purpose, this thesis helps select and direct the kind of material needed for a specific piece of writing and the ways in which that material can be shaped, organized, and presented.

What is the purpose of a player facing a fifteen-foot putt? To sink the ball in the cup is not his purpose; it's his hope. What he confronts is *how* to make the shot. He studies the pitch of the green, carefully observes the grass, notices wind currents, and plans the flight of his ball. Then, and only then, is his *purpose* clear: to tap the ball so that it will steadily follow a purposeful, predetermined path to the cup.

A logical first step in writing anything is to examine carefully the subject or topic you are going to handle. You need to know what it involves and what you propose to do with it.

About any piece of planned writing ask these four questions:

1. What special characteristics distinguish my subject?
2. Precisely what am I trying to do with it?
3. For what readers am I developing it?
4. How can I best convey my purpose and meaning to them?

Before beginning "actual writing," state in a single sentence your controlling idea, your central purpose. (This sentence may or may not be included in the finished piece of writing.) Such a sentence may be called a "statement of intent" or "thesis" or "purpose statement." Whatever it is called, it will help you to grasp, identify, and control purpose as you begin, continue, and complete the writing of whatever you have undertaken.

For example, assume that you now have a part-time job. You may be a housewife with extra time on your hands and a need for additional income. Or you may be a worker who has retired from his lifetime job and has found that retirement is boring. Or you may be a college student or teacher with long vacations during the school year and in the summer. Further assume that your experiences in finding a job may be of interest and aid to others similarly situated. You decide to write an article on part-time employment. After considerable thinking and preplanning, you might come up with a scheme like this:

General subject: Part-time Work
Limited Subject: How I Got a Part-time Job
Possible Title: I Earn and Learn
Reader: A next-door neighbor (or other teacher, retired worker, college student, or housewife)
Thesis Sentence: Part-time work can be secured by those who apply sensibly and use a carefully planned approach.

This analysis of subject is incomplete, but it does reveal a clearly stated purpose: the writer, through an account of his own experiences, can show some other identified person or persons how he or she might go about getting a part-time job.

And yet this purpose is primarily a statement of intent. It requires development. The next move is to make an inventory of what you know about the topic from personal experience and what you will need to find out. A resulting list might consist of a series of items arranged in no particular order:

1. Qualifications (health, age, sex, education) for getting a job
2. Timing the campaign
3. Discovering job opportunities (want ads, government bulletins, etc.)
4. People who can help (recommendations, testimonials)
5. Use of supporting letters
6. Making an application
7. Preparation for interview
8. Carrying out the interview
9. Difficulties in being interviewed
10. Following up job prospects

Such a listing provides an overview and suggests details to leave out. After studying it, you might decide that your central purpose should be limited to a discussion of how to find out about available jobs (No. 3) or about the terrors and rewards of being interviewed (Nos. 7–9). If you make such a decision, you would then revise your title and your thesis sentence. Limiting a subject to manageable proportions is one desirable result of setting down developing details, a process essential in all pre-planning and fixing of purpose.

Of course, after limiting a subject and stating a central purpose, you need to select a method of development that will most clearly and interestingly accomplish the purpose of your thesis sentence for your chosen readers. Some topics require a definition of terms and a serious approach. Others might require argument: facts, proof, reasons for or against this or that action or cause. For an essay such as that suggested on part-time employment, the best method might be an informal, narrative treatment.

A major aim of preplanning (Step Two) is to discover and define purpose. To select a topic, narrow it to a subtopic, and decide how to treat that subtopic is to define purpose.

There is no such thing as good *purposeless* writing.

STEP FOUR

Try to
Think Straight

Three basic problems are involved in all writing: getting ideas, getting material, and writing. These closely related acts may be expressed as two: (1) discovering who we are and how, why, and what we think about people, ideas, events, and places and (2) communicating our thoughts to our readers. The first of these steps is thinking; the second is writing. The two are inseparably linked. No one can think without using language. No one should attempt to write without genuine thought.

Oliver Wendell Holmes, the great jurist, once wrote: "A word is the skin of a living thought." Our thinking can be no better than our word supply; our writing can be no better than our thinking.

"We do not think enough about thinking, and much of our confusion is the result of current illusions in regard to it." This is the first sentence in a famous essay entitled "On Various Kinds of Thinking," by James Harvey Robinson. Perhaps we do not think enough about thinking because thinking is hard work, because we seem to get along fairly well without doing much of it, possibly because we think we are thinking when actually we are doing nothing of the sort. "If you make people *think* they're thinking," once wrote Don Marquis, an American humorist, "they'll love you. If you make them *think*, they'll hate you."

Errors in thinking can destroy fact-finding papers. They can ruin articles and speeches and reports that try to prove a point or establish a case. Each of us is only too ready to twist, ignore, or exaggerate evidence. Some errors in thinking violate that rare and valuable commodity, common sense. Other errors involve logic. The three suggestions that follow should help in checking on one's quotas of common sense and logic.

TRY TO MAKE YOUR STATEMENTS REASONABLE

"Since the beginning of time, no person has ever been reasonable at all times and in all circumstances." Most of us, perhaps all of us, would accept this as a true statement. But is it? Can we *prove* it?

It is all very well to recommend that every statement be reasonable, but this is a counsel of perfection. Reasoning is based upon facts or what are considered facts. But, for example, the *facts* of medicine or physics even ten years ago are hardly the *facts* today. Reasoning is also based upon conclusions drawn from facts. Yet the conclusions one reasonable man draws from a given set of facts may differ widely from those of another man.

Clearly, you cannot make every statement reasonable. But at least you can avoid making statements which are obviously questionable; if you do make such a statement, you should be prepared to try to prove it. You should attempt to make your meaning clear by offering evidence which might be considered factual. You can avoid statements based on faulty premises, those based on false analogy, those involving mere generalizations. How logical are these statements?

All automobiles should have governors limiting their speed to 40 miles an hour. (What about police cars? Ambulances? Fire trucks?)

Since football is the most dangerous of all sports, my parents refused to allow me to play it when I was a youngster. (Overlook the possible parental muddleheadedness: What about water polo? Bullfighting? Skin diving?)

Ted knows all there is to know about stocks and bonds. (All? Absolutely nothing he doesn't know?)

Gambling is a bad habit; everyone should avoid it because

habits are bad. (Can you prove gambling is a bad habit? Are habits bad? All habits? What about the habit of paying your debts? Saying your prayers? Telling the truth?)

If you feel that you would *never* write such unreasonable and illogical statements as these, then perhaps you do have a reasonable, logical mind. If so, you will especially appreciate this quotation from *Alice's Adventures in Wonderland*: "Contrariwise," continued Tweedledee, "if it was so, it might be; and if it were so, it would be; but if it isn't, it ain't. That's logic."

DEFINE TERMS THAT MAY NOT BE CLEAR

You should never consider your reader entirely ignorant, but if you know enough to write about a subject you know details which your reader does not. Certain terms familiar to you may be unknown to your reader. Even in context, he may be unable to guess the meaning of certain expressions. A reader should look up words he cannot define, but it is unwise to assume that he will always do so. Some slovenly readers never look up anything. Could this mean you, too?

You should define technical words for the general reader. If you use such terms as *bibb*, *idocrase*, *pegmatite*, and *tufa*, you should immediately define them; not one reader in a thousand will know what you are writing about, although each of those words is included in standard desk dictionaries. In fact, not all readers will understand even more commonly used words like *boldface*, *ecumenical*, *civil rights*, *exodontia*, and *logistics*. Always consider for whom you are writing: you need not explain *abscissa* if you believe your readers have studied trigonometry.

Even more common words than these can cause confusion. What do you mean and what will your reader understand by *normal person, low income, freedom of speech, typical professor, un-American*? It is unwise to assume that the reader will have a conception like your own of the precise meaning of such terms.

A common-sense thought for every writer is this: a word or term does not necessarily mean what the writer thinks it means, but it always means what the reader thinks it does. Arthur

Schopenhauer, the German philosopher and writer, expressed this thought clearly:

A writer commits the error of subjectivity when he thinks it enough if he himself knows what he means and wants to say, and takes no thought of the reader, who is left to get at the bottom of it as best he may. This is as though the author were holding a monologue; whereas it ought to be a dialogue, too, in which he must express himself all the more clearly inasmuch as he cannot hear the questions of his interlocutor. The words should be so set down that they directly force the reader to think precisely the same thing as the author thought when he wrote them. Nor will this result be obtained unless the author has always been careful to remember that thought so far follows the law of gravity that it travels from head to paper much more readily than from paper to head; so that he must assist the latter passage by every means in his power.

WATCH OUT FOR LOGICAL LOOPHOLES

Two common methods of thinking, used and abused every day, are *induction* and *deduction*. The former seeks to establish a general truth, an all embracing principle or conclusion. The inductive process begins by using observation of specific facts; it classifies these facts, looks for similarities among them, and from what may be considered a sufficient number of these facts or particulars draws a conclusion or "leads into" a principle. Movement of thought is always from the particular to the general.

Deduction seeks to establish a specific conclusion by showing that it conforms to or "leads down from" a general truth or principle. Movement of thought, expressed or implied, is from the general to the particular.

In other words, induction is the process of thinking by which one generalizes from particulars; deduction is that form of reasoning wherein we put ideas together to see what can be inferred from them. In induction, one reasons from facts to generalizations; in deduction, one reasons from premises (propositions, assumptions) to conclusions. The premises involved in deduction may be the product of inductive reasoning and therefore rooted in fact, but investigation of fact is not part of the deductive process itself.

Processes of thought such as these may seem different from any thinking of which you consider yourself capable, but look at this example. Early in history, men became convinced that no one lives forever, that sooner or later everyone dies. Through inductive thinking, mankind arrived at a general conclusion: "All men are mortal." A generalization so well established as this needs no further testing or reexamination and may be used as a starting point, or premise, in deductive thinking. Thus in the form of a syllogism we examine the future of a man named Ned Sloan:

Major premise: All men are mortal.
Minor premise: Ned Sloan is a man.
Conclusion: Ned Sloan is mortal.

We reason much this way, although we do not usually arrange thoughts in a formal syllogism. For example, we assume that events in the future will resemble those encountered in the past. What is the real meaning of "A burnt child dreads the fire"?

In induction, the possibility of exceptions exists, but general conclusions reached by inductive processes are usually valid. When you write "Most hard-working people get ahead" the statement will be acceptable to most readers, although there are exceptions and although you cannot possibly have examined all records and cannot be positive about the future. The inductive conclusion that no two people have identical fingerprints is reasonable, although the statement is only theoretically capable of being positively proved.

Through inductive reasoning, the laws (that is, the principles, the generalized and descriptive statements) of any science, such as biology, chemistry, and physics, have been arrived at. Through deductive reasoning they are applied in particular situations: the launching of a space rocket, the manufacture of a computer, the development of a vaccine. In pure and applied

science, such reasoning is virtually foolproof. But loopholes
do occur where human beings and human behavior are
directly concerned.

Here is brief comment on the nine most common everyday
offenses against straight and clear thinking:

1. Hasty generalization

The most prevalent error in inductive reasoning is observing
only a few instances and then jumping to an unwarranted conclusion. For instance, you know a few athletes whom you consider stupid; does it follow that all, or even most, athletes are
mentally deficient? What is the inductive evidence for labeling
certain groups "teen-age gangsters," "irresponsible women
drivers," "absent-minded professors," "male chauvinist pigs,"
"dumb blondes"? What is the evidence for "every schoolboy
knows . . ." or "all good Americans realize . . ." or "statistics
show . . ."? Fundamental honesty, common sense, and your
own personal responsibility should prevent loose and unwarranted conclusions.

2. Non sequitur

The major error in deductive thinking is the "it does not
follow" assumption. *Non sequitur* is an inference or conclusion
that does not proceed from the premises or materials upon
which it is apparently based. This fallacy can be caused by a
false major premise and by a minor premise which is only apparently related to the major premise. For example, some good
professional writers admit to being poor spellers. Are you
justified in concluding that you, too, also a poor speller, are
destined to be a good professional writer?

3. Post hoc, ergo propter hoc

This term, a name applied to a variation of "hasty generalization," means "after this, therefore on account of this." It involves
a mistake in thinking which holds that a happening coming
before another must necessarily or naturally be its cause or that,
when one event follows another, the latter event is the result of

the first. "I have a cold today because I sat in a draft yesterday." "No wonder this happened to me; I walked under a ladder yesterday." "The Roman Empire fell after the birth and spread of Christianity." Those who seriously argue—and many have— that Christianity alone directly caused the downfall of Rome commit the *post hoc, ergo propter hoc* error in reasoning.

4. Biased or suppressed evidence

Evidence consists of facts which furnish grounds for belief and that help to prove an assumption, premise, or proposition. A serious flaw in basic honesty and in thinking is selecting evidence from questionable sources or leaving out evidence that runs contrary to the point the writer wishes to make. The testimony of dedicated club members is not in itself sufficient to prove that club membership promotes good fellowship or a happy social life. What do non-members think? What is the evidence of club members who do not especially value their membership?

Figures and statistics can be made to lie if evidence is biased or suppressed. Many so-called truths have been prepared by paid propagandists and by directly interested individuals and groups. This flaw in reasoning has led many people to recognize that "figures don't lie, but liars figure."

5. Distinguishing fact from opinion

A fact is based on actuality of some sort; it is a verifiable statement or event. An opinion is a conclusion or inference that may be mingled with a supposed fact. That William Faulkner was "an American writer" is a statement based on actuality which can be positively proved. That Faulkner was "the greatest American novelist of the twentieth century" is only an opinion of those who hold it. That Thomas Jefferson was President from 1801 until the inauguration of James Madison in 1809 is a fact; that Jefferson was "our greatest President" is a matter of opinion. A favorite device of many writers and speakers is to mingle opinions with facts and thus obscure the difference between them.

6. Begging the question

This flaw in thinking consists of taking a conclusion for granted before it is proved or assuming in the propositions (premises) that which is to be proved in the conclusion. A question such as "Should a vicious man like C. Melvin Jones be allowed to hold office?" is "loaded" because it assumes what needs to be proved.

Common forms of "begging the question" are *slanting, name calling,* and *shifting the meaning of a word.*

Using suggestive words to create an emotional attitude (as in the application of "vicious" to C. Melvin Jones, above) is a form of slanting. It is also a form of *argumentum ad hominem,* a Latin phrase meaning "argument against the person." That is, it is an argument against the person who may hold an opinion rather than against the opinion itself: "Only an idiot would believe that."

Guard against using or fully believing such suggestive words and phrases as "bigoted," "saintly," "progressive," "reactionary," "undemocratic ideas," "dangerous proposal." Use them if you have supporting evidence; accept them if the proof offered seems valid and thorough. Otherwise, avoid slanting in writing and be on guard when reading and listening.

Name calling is allied to slanting. It appeals to prejudice and emotion rather than to the intellect. It employs "good" words to approve and accept, "bad" words to condemn and reject. In writing and reading, be cautious in using such terms as "angel in disguise," "rabble rouser," "benefactor," etc.

Shifting the meaning of a word consists of using the same word several times with a shift in meaning designed to confuse the reader or listener. A *conservative* disposed to preserve existing conditions and to agree with gradual rather than abrupt changes is one thing; a *conservative* against all progress, a complete reactionary and mossback, is another. Should everyone vote the Republican ticket because this country is a *republic* or vote the Democratic ticket because it is a *democracy*?

7. *Evading the issue*

This error in thinking is common in arguments. It consists of ignoring the point under discussion and making a statement that has no bearing on the main issue. If you tell a friend that he drives too fast and he replies that you are a poor driver yourself, he has evaded the issue. He may be right, but he has neither met your objection nor won the argument. (Actually, he has resorted to the *ad hominem* argument mentioned above.) It is only too easy to sidestep an issue and launch a counterattack.

8. *Faulty analogy*

Because two objects or ideas are alike in one or more ways, they are not necessarily similar in some further respect. An analogy (partial similarity) can be accurate and effective; otherwise we would have no similes and metaphors. But an analogy is not designed to *prove* anything. In the kinds of writing most of us do most of the time, an analogy is chiefly used for illustration. In many analogies, differences outweigh and outnumber similarities. Suppose you are writing on the question "Why do we need Social Security?" It would be absurd to use such analogies as these: Do we help trees when they lose their leaves in heavy storms or autumn winds? Do we provide help to dogs and horses in their old age? Some tribes kill people when they are too old to be useful.

Even more literal analogies than these can be ridiculous. You may, for instance, reason that since the honor system worked well in the small high school you attended it will work equally well in the high school in which your children are now students. Are the similarities between the schools either superficial or less important than the differences? The whipping post was a deterrent to crime in seventeenth-century New England. Is it false analogy to suggest that similar punishment should be inflicted on twentieth-century criminals, dope addicts, "hippies," or "squares"?

9. *Testimonials*

Citing statements from historical personages or well-known contemporaries is not necessarily straight thinking. In an attempt to bolster an argument, we are quick to employ such terms as "Authorities have concluded," "Science proves," "Doctors say," "Laboratory tests reveal . . ." George Washington, Thomas Jefferson, and Abraham Lincoln—justly renowned as they are— might not have held economic, social, and political views necessarily valid in the twentieth century. Douglas MacArthur was a great military strategist, but something he said about combustion engines may be less convincing than the words of a good local mechanic. Is an authority in one field an oracle of wisdom about any subject on which he speaks or writes?

As a witness for or against an important foreign trade policy, how effective would an eminent surgeon be? A football hero? A TV personality? If you were writing an attack on vaccination, would you reasonably expect the cited opposition of George Bernard Shaw to outweigh the pronouncements of the entire medical profession? Thomas A. Edison was a great inventor, but you would be ill-advised to cite his odd notions about gravity. Henry Ford would not be a wise choice for you to quote in some argument about history.

But even where there is little question of the validity of authority, be careful that neither bias nor the time element weakens your presentation. Some businessmen and labor leaders are experts on economic problems, but their particular interests might prevent their having the impartiality, the objectivity, of a disinterested observer, such as a professor of economics. And even a professor might be biased in favor of some specific school of economic thought.

As for timing, remember that in many fields of human activity and knowledge, authorities may become obsolete. Charles Darwin no longer has the last word on evolution. Sigmund Freud is not universally considered the final authority in psychoanalysis.

Logic is the rule by which we evaluate the statements and

arguments of others, especially when our common sense and skeptical minds have already made us suspicious. Logic is also the rule by which we measure our own thinking.

It requires effort—but not in any great amount—to turn unconscious thinking and plain common sense into conscious reasoning. Small though it be, this effort may be the most important of all steps toward better writing.

STEP FIVE

Choose and Use Words Carefully

Important as they are, you may unwisely consider the first four suggested steps to better writing as being preliminary, kinds of warming-up exercises. They aren't. Regardless of your opinions, however, you will agree that, as ordinarily thought of, writing "begins" with words. This fifth step deals with the choice and use of words for the expression of ideas, that is, *diction*. (The term *diction* comes from Latin "dictio," meaning "word" or "saying." The root *dict* is familiar to us in words like *dictator*, *dictionary*, *dictate*, and *Dictaphone*.)

Because there are many words to choose from, because many ideas require expression in different shades of meaning and emphasis, and because errors should be avoided, diction is troublesome for all writers and speakers.

Diction should be *correct*, *clear*, and *effective*, but no standards can be absolute. Our language is constantly changing. Also, diction, like fashions in dress and food, is influenced by changes in taste. Again, what is acceptable in daily speech and conversation may not be suitable in written form. The use of this or that word cannot be justified by saying that it is often heard or seen in print. Advertisements, newspapers, magazines, and even some books exhibit faulty diction.

Common problems in choosing and using words may be summarized as follows:

(1.) Words should be in *current* use.
(2.) Words should be in *national* use.

(3.) Words should be in *reputable* use.
(4.) Words should be *exact and emphatic*.

CURRENT USE

The first requirement of good usage is that words must be understandable to readers and listeners of the present time. Words do go out of style and out of use. Except for doubtful purposes of humor, avoid antiquated expressions.

OBSOLETE WORDS

An *obsolete* word is one that has completely passed out of use; an *obsolescent* word is one in the process of becoming obsolete. One dictionary may label a word as "obsolete," another may call the same word "archaic." Does your dictionary include *infortune* for *misfortune, garb* for *personal bearing, prevent* for *precede, anon* for *coming*?

ARCHAIC WORDS

An *archaic* word is an old-fashioned word, one that has passed from ordinary language, although it may still appear in legal and Biblical expressions. Avoid using expressions such as these: *enow* for *enough, gramercy* for *thank you, methinks* for *it seems to me, lief* for *willing, oft* or *ofttimes* for *often, wot* for *know, whilom* for *formerly, bedight* for *array*.

POETIC WORDS

Words that have been (and are still occasionally) used in poetry but not in prose are known as *poetic diction*. Since early in the nineteenth century, much poetic diction has been imaginative combinations of words rather than isolated words themselves.

"Poetic" words, sometimes so designated in dictionaries, are usually archaic words found in poetry composed in or intended to create the aura of a remote past. Examples are contractions such as *'tis, 'twas*; the use of *-st, -est, -th, -eth* endings on present-tense verbs: *dost, would'st, doth, leadeth*; and words like *'neath, ope,* and *glebe.*

NEOLOGISMS

A *neologism* is a newly coined word or phrase or an established word or phrase employed in a new meaning. Not all neologisms are contrived and artificial, but the majority are. Several well-known columnists and broadcasters repeatedly concoct neologisms. So do many sports commentators and advertising copywriters. Their productions are frequently colorful, attention-getting, and picturesque, but only a few of them prove permanently valuable.

New words are coined in various ways. Some are adaptations of common words: *millionheiress*. Some, the so-called portmanteau words, are combinations of common words: *brunch* (*br*eakfast and *l*unch), *smog* (*sm*oke and f*og*), *slanguage* (*slang* and *language*). Some are formed from the initial letters of common words: *loran* (*lo*ng *ra*nge *n*avigation), *radar* (*ra*dio *d*etecting *a*nd *r*anging). Some are virtually new formations, like *gobbledygook*, modeled on the meaningless sounds made by a turkey. Some are comparatively unknown, despite their creation by eminent writers: *clouderpuffs* (a sky full of round soft clouds), by Conrad Aiken; *popaganda* (Father's Day), by Edward Anthony; *globilliterate* (one ignorant of world affairs), by Norman Corbin.

Discoveries, new inventions, and occupations inspire new coinages: *A-bomb, rhombatron, realtor, beautician*. Registered trade names or trademarks are in the same classification: *Dacron, Technicolor, Kodak*.

New words that appear in dictionaries may have no label or be labeled "slang" or "colloquial." (Some neologisms, like *motel*, change to permanent status and become common words.) Until a "new" word is widely accepted in present (current) use, it is best to avoid using it. Like some slang, most neologisms are "here today, gone tomorrow." How recently have you heard or read such neologisms as *cinemaddict* (lover of films), *aristobrat* (son or daughter of rich parents), *publicator* (press agent), and *tube steak* (the hot dog)?

NATIONAL USE

Words and expressions understandable to us may, to others, be localisms, technical terms, shoptalk, or untranslatable foreign expressions. Also, idiomatic expressions acceptable in one part of the country may not be understood elsewhere. If you use such expressions as the following in speech and writing, drop them from your vocabulary, unless they are needed for some definite stylistic effect: the localisms *calculate*, *reckon*, and *guess* (for think or suppose); such semi-technical words as *half-volley*, *eagle*, *double steal*, *full gainer*, *birdie*, *switch tacks* (unless these terms are used in direct reference to various sports); such Anglicisms as *bonnet* (hood of a car), *biscuits* (cookies), *bowler* (derby), and *lift* (elevator).

Actually, if English is to remain a world language, it is important that words have not only national, but international, acceptance. Some observers have mentioned that we have, among many varieties, what might be called "Oxford English," "Australian English," and "New York English." When Confucius was asked what his first deed would be if he were to be made Emperor of China, he replied, "I would reestablish the precise meaning of words." Such an aim was impossible then and is impossible now. The difficulty of worldwide acceptance of word meanings is illustrated by this remark: "I was mad about my flat." In England it means "I liked my apartment"; in the United States it would usually mean "I was angry because I had a punctured tire."

An Americanism such as *lickety-split* is more vivid and picturesque than "fast" or "rapid," but its meaning might be unclear in Wales, South Africa, or New Zealand. Even in our own country, the problem is not always simple. Would everyone understand this sign posted in a North Carolina country store:

"Kwittin credit till I get my outins in"? To those who can translate, however, the sentence is more quaint and expressive than "I shall extend no further credit to anyone who has not made full payment for goods already received." And consider this sign tacked onto a door in Pennsylvania Dutch country: "Button don't bell. Bump." This vivid, quaint message means "Please knock because the bell is out of order."

INAPPROPRIATE LOCALISMS

A *localism* is a word or phrase used and understood in a particular section or region. It may also be called a *regionalism* or a *provincialism*.

The western, southwestern, southern, and northeastern areas of the United States are rich in localisms that add flavor to speech but that may not be understood in other areas. Such expressions are difficult for a native of one of these areas to detect: as a writer or speaker he accepts them as reputable and assumes them to be generally understood, since he himself has known and used them from childhood. Although such words and combinations of words may not always be explained in print, dictionaries do label or define many words according to the geographical area where they are common. Examples:

Western: *grubstake* (supplies or funds furnished a prospector), *coulee* (narrow, steep-walled valley), *rustler* (cattle thief), *dogie, dogy* (motherless calf), *sagebrush* (a flower of the aster family).

Southwest: *mesa* (flat-topped rocky hill with steeply sloping sides), *mustang* (small, hardy, half-wild horse), *longhorn* (formerly a variety of cattle), *mesquite* (spiny tree or shrub), *maverick* (an unbranded animal).

South: *butternuts* (a kind of brown overalls), *granny* (a nurse), *lightwood* (pitchy pine wood), *corn pone* (corn bread), *hoecake* (a cake of Indian meal), *chunk* (throw), *tote* (carry), *poke* (sack).

Northeastern: *down-easter* (a native of New England, especially of Maine), *selectman* (a town official), *choose* (wish).

INAPPROPRIATE NATIONALISMS

An extension of localism is *nationalism*, a term describing expressions common in or limited to English used by one of the English-speaking nations. *Americanism* and *Briticism* refer to words or word meanings common, respectively, in the United States and in the British Isles; logically, other labels might be *Canadianisms*, *Australianisms*, *New-Zealandisms*, and *South Africanisms*.

Americanisms: *catchup* (tomato sauce); *levee* (an embankment); *calaboose* (prison, jail); *stump* (travel to electioneer); *bellhop*; *caboose*; *gangster*; *haberdasher*; *gusher*.
Briticisms: *accumulator* (storage battery); *tube* (subway); *croft* (small enclosed field); *petrol* (gasoline), *stay-in strike* (sit-down strike).
Scotch dialect: *bairn* (child); *canty* (cheerful); *auld* (old); *bree* (broth); *awee* (a little while).

Advice to avoid inappropriate nationalisms does not apply to American words and phrases but to those of other English-speaking countries when such words and phrases would not be readily understood in your writing.

INAPPROPRIATE SHOPTALK

The specialized or technical vocabulary and idioms of those in the same work or the same way of life are known as *shoptalk*, the language people use in discussing their particular line of activity. To *talk shop* is the verb form of this expression.

Avoid introducing into writing words and expressions peculiar to, or understood only by, members of a particular profession, trade, science, or art. Legal jargon, medical jargon, and sports jargon, for example, have special meanings for people in those particular fields or occupations. So do more than forty other classifications of words that have special subject labels: *astronomy*, *entomology*, *psychology*, *engineering*, and so on. Examples of technical words are *sidereal* (astronomy), *broadside* (nautical), *lepidopterous*, (zoology). Some have crept into popular use: *telescope* (astronomy), *virtuoso* (music and art), *stereo* (sound reproduction), *analog computer* (electronics).

A specialist writing for specialists uses many technical words. If he is writing for others in the same general field, he will use fewer technical terms, or less difficult ones, and will define the more specialized terms. If he is writing for the nonspecialist and the general reader, he will use no technical terms at all or will define the ones he does use.

OVERUSE OF FOREIGN WORDS AND PHRASES

For Americans, a foreign word or phrase is one from a non-English language. Tens of thousands of foreign words have come into our language from Greek, Latin, and French, and thousands more have come from other languages. Depending upon your dictionary, you will find from 40 to 150 foreign-language abbreviations used for word origins and meanings.

Two things happen to these foreign words and phrases: (1) If they have been widely used or used over a long period, or both, they are Anglicized and become a part of our everyday language, recorded in dictionaries like any common word. (2) If the conditions of (1) have not been met, the word or phrase remains foreign: as such, it is indicated in dictionaries as foreign, partly as a guide for a writer to use italics if he uses the word or phrase. Anglicized examples: a priori, à la mode, blitz, chef, habitué, smorgasbord. Non-Anglicized examples: *Anno Domini, fait accompli, cause célèbre, ex libris, mañana, Weltschmerz.*

Use common sense in employing foreign words and phrases. If the word or phrase has been Anglicized or if no good English equivalent exists, use it. But why *merci beaucoup* for "thank you" or *Auf Wiedersehen* for "good-by"? Even *a* or *an* serves better than *per*: "$5 *an* hour." Do not use such foreign expressions merely to impress the reader.

REPUTABLE USE

A writer's vocabulary is the *number* of words he can command; a writer's diction is the *kind* of words he uses. The first, most important, and fairest test of a word is usage. But usage must be "reputable"; that is, in diction one should follow standards set by that large body of accomplished speakers and writers who we have reason to believe know the language best. These standards rule out a number of words that most of us have in our vocabularies. In compensating for their loss, however, we may fall into errors. That is, in substituting reputable expressions for disreputable ones, we may forget that the *primary* purpose of all writing is communication and that usage must be appropriate as well as reputable.

COLLOQUIALISMS

A *colloquialism* is a conversational word or phrase permissible in, and often indispensable to, an easy, informal style of speaking and writing. A colloquialism is not substandard, not illiterate; it is an expression more often used in speech than in writing and more appropriate in informal than formal speech and writing. The origin of the word is Latin *colloquium*, for "conversation." Our word *colloquy* means "speaking together"; the word *loquacious* means "given to talking, fond of talking."

Dictionary words and phrases are marked as colloquial (*Colloq.*) when the editors judge them to be more common in speech than in writing or more suitable in informal than formal discourse. A large number of words and phrases are so labeled. The term applies to many expressions because informal English has a wide range and because editors differ in interpretations of their findings. Certain contractions, such as *don't*, *shouldn't*, and *won't* are considered "acceptable" colloquialisms; others, however, such as *'tis*, *'twas*, *'twere*, should be avoided in even informal writing. No objective rule or test will tell you when to use a colloquialism and when not to. In general, use a colloquialism when your writing would otherwise seem stiff and artificial.

The following are examples of colloquialisms (as in dictionaries and linguistic studies, no attempt is made to indicate their comparative rank): angel (financial backer), brass (impudence), freeze (stand motionless), don't, jinx, enthuse, phone, ad, gumption, cute, hasn't got any, brass tacks (facts), show up, try and, take a try at, alongside of, flabbergast, fizzle, flop, root for, make out, fill the bill.

You might use any or all of these colloquialisms if you are reporting the conversation of a person who would characteristically speak them. You might use one or more of them in informal writing where the tone is light or humorous or breezy. But if you use any colloquialisms at all, use only a few and be certain that they are in keeping with the purpose and tone of your writing.

SLANG

Slang is a label for a particular kind of colloquialism.

Characteristics of slang include flippant or eccentric humor; forced, fantastic, or grotesque meanings; novelty; attempts to be colorful, fresh, and vivid. Such expressions may capture the popular fancy or some segment of it (college slang, musical slang, baseball slang), but in the main they are substandard. Even so, slang may for a while be used over a broad area, and a large number of words and phrases bear the "slang" label in dictionaries. If such expressions survive, they may in time receive the respectable label "colloquial." Some of the following examples appear in dictionaries with the "slang" label; some may appear there eventually; and some will not appear at all, because their vogue is too short-lived.

Neologisms (newly coined words): *scrumptious, wacky, shyster, mooch, beatnik, razz, oops, hornswoggle, goofy, payola, scram, nix, teenybopper, pizzaz.* (Not all newly coined words, however, are slang.)

Words formed from others by abbreviation or by adding endings to change the part of speech: *VIP* (*V*ery *I*mportant Person), *psych out, groovy, snafu, phony, chintzy, nervy, mod.*

Words in otherwise acceptable use given extended meanings:
*chicken, grind, corny, guts, lousy, swell, buck, bean, jerk,
square, guy, grub, sack, blow, grease, touch, cat, fuzz, pad.*

Words formed by compounding or coalescing two or more
words: *whodunit, stash* (*store* and *cache*), *egghead, high-
hat, attaboy* (that's the boy), *screwball.*

Phrases made up of one or more newly coined words (neologisms) and one or more acceptable ones: *goof off, pork
barrel, blow one's top, bum steer, shoot the bull, live it up,
deadbeat, have a ball, off one's rocker, conk out, jam ses-
sion, cut out, shoot the works, cool it.*

Slang, although popular, has little place in formal writing or
even in effective informal writing. First, many slang words and
expressions last for a brief time and then pass out of use, becoming unintelligible to many readers and listeners. Second,
using slang expressions keeps you from searching for the exact
words you need to convey your meaning. To refer to a person
as a "creep" hardly expresses exactly or fully any critical judgment or intelligent description. Third, slang does not serve the
primary aim of writing: conveying a clear and exact message
from writer to reader. Finally, slang is not suitable in most
formal or careful informal writing because it is not in keeping
with the context. Words should be appropriate to the audience,
the occasion, and the subject.

There are, however, some arguments in favor of slang in
certain situations. It does express feeling. It also makes effective
short cuts in expression and often prevents artificiality in writing.
Furthermore, it should be used in recording dialogue to convey
the flavor of speech actually used.

IDIOMATIC USAGE

English *idiom* or *idiomatic* English concerns words used in
combination with others. Of Greek origin, the word *idiom* meant
"a private citizen, something belonging to a private citizen,
personal," and, by extension, something individual and peculiar.

Idiomatic expressions, then, conform to no laws or principles describing their formation. An idiomatic expression may violate grammar or logic or both and still be acceptable because the phrase is familiar, deep-rooted, widely used, and easily understandable—for the native born. "How do you do?" is, for example, an accepted idiom, although an exact answer would be absurd.

A few generalized statements may be made about the many idiomatic expressions in our language. One is that several words combined may lose their literal meaning and express something only remotely suggested by any one word: *birds of a feather, blacklist, lay up, toe the line, make out, bed of roses, dark horse, heavy hand, open house, read between the lines, no ax to grind, hard row to hoe.*

A second statement about idioms is that parts of the human body have suggested many of them: *burn one's fingers, all thumbs, fly in the face of, stand on one's own feet, keep body and soul together, keep one's eyes open, step on someone's toes, rub elbows with, get one's back up, keep one's chin up.*

A third generalization is that hundreds of idiomatic phrases contain adverbs or prepositions with other parts of speech. Here are some examples: *walk off, walk over, walk-up; run down, run in, run off, run out; get nowhere, get through, get off.*

agree	*to* a proposal
	on a plan
	with a person
contend	*for* a principle
	with a person
	against an obstacle
differ	*with* a person
	from something else
	about or *over* a question
impatient	*for* something desired
	with someone else
	of restraint
	at someone's conduct

> *rewarded* *for* something done
>   *with* a gift
>   *by* a person

Usage should conform to the idiomatic word combinations that are generally acceptable. A good dictionary contains explanations of idiomatic usage following key words that need such explanation, even though interpretations of particular expressions may differ from dictionary to dictionary.

EXACT AND EMPHATIC DICTION

Some (perhaps many) of the words you speak and write may be in current, national, and reputable use and yet be neither exact nor effective.

The exact use of words depends upon *clear thinking*. If we have only a vague idea, we are likely to choose for its expression the first words that come to mind. But if we know *exactly* what we have in mind, we will search for the word or words that will most accurately express what we mean to say.

For example, consider one of the overworked words in our language, *pretty*. We speak of a pretty girl, a pretty flower, a pretty day, and so on. The word *pretty* carries a somewhat general meaning and cannot be called incorrect. But does it express exactly what we mean to convey? Perhaps it would be more accurate to say that a certain girl is *attractive*, or *beautiful*, or *personable*, or *charming*, or *exquisite*, or *fair*, or *sensuous*, or *dainty*, or *engaging*. These words are not all synonyms for *pretty*, but perhaps one of them would more exactly express an impression than the now trite and ineffective *pretty*.

To determine the exact word needed, you must become aware of shades of meaning, of distinctions that clarify the idea for which you wish to use the word as symbol. When you want to describe a surface that, from every point of view, lies on a line corresponding to or parallel with the horizon, will you use *flat*, *plane*, *level*, *even*, *flush*, or *smooth*? Always choose the word that shows most exactly the meaning you intend.

Sometimes the first word that comes to mind is the most nearly exact which can be used; more often it is not. Also, remember that a word means to the reader what the reader thinks it means, not necessarily what the writer thinks.

Again, a word may be exact and yet be lacking in force, animation, and strength. It is reasonably "exact" to refer to a dog as being of *mixed breed* but more lively and emphatic to refer to it as a *mongrel.* Effective writing is vigorous and positive and uses colorless words only as necessary. Emphatic diction requires expressive nouns, verbs, adjectives, and adverbs.

The following sections are designed to help you make your writing and speech more exact *and* effective. As you study them, remember that not only may exact diction be unemphatic but vigorous and forceful diction may be inexact.

IMPROPRIETIES

Improprieties are recognized (standard) English words misused in function or meaning. One classification of improprieties includes words acceptable as one part of speech but unacceptable as another: nouns improperly substituted for verbs, verbs for nouns, adjectives for nouns, adjectives for adverbs, adverbs for adjectives, prepositions for conjunctions. Another includes misuses of principal parts of verbs. Such improprieties have been called "coined grammar."

A word identified as more than one part of speech may be so used without question, but a word should not be moved from one part of speech and placed in another until standard usage has sanctioned this new function. Examples of grammatical improprieties:

> *Nouns used as verbs:* grassing a lawn, *suppering,* to *party,* *passengered,* to *suspicion,* to *suicide*
> *Verbs used as nouns:* eats, a *repeat,* a *sell, advise,* an *invite*
> *Adjectives used as adverbs:* dances *good, awful* short, *real* pretty
> *Verb forms:* come for *came, don't* for *doesn't, done* for *did, hadn't ought, set* for *sit, of* for *have, seen* for *saw.*

Another classification of improprieties includes words similar to other words and used inaccurately in their place. Such words include homonyms and homographs. *Homonyms* are two words that have the same or almost the same pronunciation, but are different in meaning, in origin, and frequently in spelling; for example, *real* and *reel*; *made* and *maid*; *hour, our,* and *are*; *accept, except.*

Homographs are two or more words that have the same spelling but are different in meaning, origin, and perhaps pronunciation. Examples: *slaver* (a dealer in slaves) and *slaver* (drool or drivel); *arms* (parts of the body) and *arms* (weapons); *bat* (club, cudgel) and *bat* (flying rodent). Homographs cannot cause misspelling, but they can cause confusion or ambiguity.

Near-homonyms may also cause confusion: *farther* for *further, father* for *further, genial* for *general, stationary* for *stationery, morass* for *morose, loose* for *lose, imminent* for *eminent, aisle* for *isle, allude* for *elude, climactic* for *climatic.*

SPECIFIC AND GENERAL WORDS

A specific word names a narrow concept; a general word names a broad concept. *House* is a general word, whereas *castle, chalet, lodge, mansion, hut, shack,* and *villa* are specific. A *red* dress may be *carnelian, cerise, crimson, magenta, scarlet,* or *vermilion.* A conventional verb such as *walk* is general; more specific (and occasionally more effective) are such words as *flounce, mince, prance, saunter, shamble, stagger, stride, stroll, strut, totter,* and *traipse.*

Specific words are more exact and usually more effective than general words, but writing can become overloaded with highly charged concepts. The second of the following sentences is more exact and emphatic than the first, but it is too specific to be genuinely effective:

There was an old boat moving through the heavy sea.

Like a lady wrestler among thieves, the tanker *Isobel Ann* lunged into each massive green wave and, with a grunt of ancient rage, flung the Arctic-spawned monster over her scaling brown shoulder.

CONCRETE AND ABSTRACT WORDS

A concrete word expresses something tangible, usually perceivable by one or more of the senses: *encrusted, forsythia, gargle, guillotine, lemony, waddle*. An abstract word suggests no really tangible image or impression: *duty, honor, leave, move, persuasion, slow, truth*.

Concrete words are specific, and specific words are frequently concrete; abstract words are general, and general words are often abstract. Ordinarily, and within reason, choose the specific, concrete word over the general, abstract one.

EXAGGERATION

Exaggeration is the act of magnifying, overstating, and going beyond the limits of truth. In writing, exaggeration is used to intensify or strengthen meaning: *starved* or *famished* for "hungry," *a million thanks, abject adoration*.

In most instances, exaggeration actually misrepresents and is neither exact nor effective: "I thought I'd die laughing." Exaggeration occasionally may be used effectively, but it is more often misleading. Be on guard when using such words as *amazing, awful, fantastic, gorgeous, horrible, marvelous, overwhelming, staggering, terrible, thrilling, tremendous*, and *wonderful*.

AFFECTATION

Affectation is artificial behavior designed to impress others, a mannerism for effect that involves some kind of show or pretense. In language, it is evident in the use of words and expressions not customary or appropriate for the speaker or writer employing them. Getting rid of words and expressions that are not reputable and simultaneously trying to increase the vigor and appeal of one's speech and writing are worthwhile endeavors. Deliberately trying to be different or learned or impressive often results in misinterpretation, confusion, and annoyance. Pretense is a greater sin against expressive English than even "bad grammar."

For example, a recent magazine article contained this paragraph:

> The opportunity for options in life distinguishes the rich from the poor. Perhaps through better motivation, the upper levels of the poor could be tempted onto the option track. It is important to motivate such people close to breakthrough level in income because they are closest to getting a foot on the option ladder.

What this writer probably meant was "The more money you have, the more choices you have." He used reputable expressions, but he fell into the greater error of affectation.

EUPHEMISMS

A *euphemism* is a softened, bland, inoffensive expression used instead of one that may suggest something unpleasant. In avoiding the use of such nonreputable expressions as *croak*, *kick the bucket*, and *take the last count*, you may be tempted to write *pass away* or *depart this life*. Unless religious dictates prevent, use the short, direct word *die*. Other examples of euphemisms to be avoided: *prevaricate* for *lie*, *watery plain* for *sea* or *ocean*, *expectorate* for *spit*, *mortician* for *undertaker*, *lowing herd* for *cattle*, *villatic fowl* for *chicken*, *separate from school* for *expel*, *abdomen* for *belly*, *love child* for *illegitimate*.

Here is a short list of expressions recently noted in magazine and newspaper articles and advertisements, together with possible translations into useful English:

preowned car (secondhand car)

senior citizens (old people)

problem skin (acne)

motion discomfort (nausea)

sanitary engineer (garbageman)

custodial engineer (janitor)

experienced tires (retreads or recaps)

collection correspondent (bill
   collector)
comfort station (public toilet)

cardiovascular accident
   (stroke)

JARGON AND GOBBLEDYGOOK

Jargon is a general term sometimes applied to mixed linguistic forms for communication between speakers who do not know each other's language—for example, *pidgin English* and *lingua franca*. It refers as well to speaking and writing that contain a number of expressions unfamiliar to the general reader (the jargon of sports, the jargon of atomic physicists) and to writing filled with long words (polysyllabication) and circumlocutions (indirect or roundabout expressions).

"Short words are words of might." This observation—wise but no truer than most generalizations—does not imply that long words should never be used; it does suggest that long words are more likely than short ones to be artificial, affected, and pretentious. The user of jargon will write "The answer is in the negative" rather than "No." For him, "worked hard" is "pursued his tasks with great diligence"; "bad weather" is "unfavorable climatic conditions"; "food" becomes "comestibles"; "fire" becomes "devouring element"; "a meal" becomes "succulent viands" or "a savory repast." The jargoneer also employs what has been called "the trick of elegant variation": he may call a spade a spade the first time but then refer to "an agricultural implement."

It is impossible always to use concrete words, but be certain you mean precisely what you say in writing such usually vague words as *asset, case, character, condition, degree, factor, instance, nature, personality, persuasion, quality, state,* and *thing.* It is likely you will never really have to use such expressions as these: *according as to whether, along the line of, in connection with,* and *in regard to.*

Gobbledygook (or *gobbledegook*) is a special kind of jargon: generally unintelligible, wordy, inflated, and obscure verbiage. Jargon is always undesirable but is often understandable; gobbledygook is likely to be meaningless or quite difficult to decipher. The word was coined by a former United States congressman, grown weary of involved government reports, who apparently had in mind the throaty sound made by a male turkey.

The term is increasingly applied to governmental and bureaucratic pronouncements that have been referred to as "masterpieces of complexity." For example, the phrase "the chance of war" in gobbledygook might be "in the regrettable eventuality of failure of the deterrence policy." But gobbledygook is not confined to bureaucratic circles. Here is a direct quotation from a financial adviser concerning shares of stock: "Overall, the underlying pattern, notwithstanding periods of consolidation, remains suggestive of at least further selective improvement over the foreseeable future." What he meant: "Selected stocks will increase in price."

A plumber, an often-told story goes, wrote to inform an agency of the United States government that he had found hydrochloric acid good for cleaning out pipes. Some bureaucrat responded with this gobbledygook: "The efficiency of hydrochloric acid is indisputable, but the corrosive residue is incompatible with metallic permanence." The plumber responded that he was glad the agency agreed. After several more such letters, an official finally wrote what he should have originally: "Don't use hydrochloric acid. It eats the inside out of pipes."

Step Five is a big one. As you will have noted, it is complex and intricate. And yet it is so important a step to better writing that you are urged to return to it again and again to "recruit the vigor" of your vocabulary.

STEP SIX

Watch Out for Tired Language

This step also deals with diction and could have been included as part of Step Five. And yet the problem of tired language is so acute, so important, and so widespread that it deserves separate treatment. Nothing is a greater offense against correct, exact, and effective word choice than the use of words and expressions that have grown stale and weary through overuse. Tired language goes by several names: triteness, hackneyed expressions, and clichés.

The words *triteness*, *hackneyed language*, and *cliché* have origins that explain their meaning. *Triteness* comes from the Latin word, *tritus*, the past participle of a verb meaning "to rub, to wear out." *Hackneyed* is derived from the idea of a horse, or carriage (hackney coach), let out for hire, devoted to common use, and consequently exhausted in service. *Cliché* comes from the French word *clicher*, meaning "to stereotype," "to cast from a mold."

Trite expressions resemble slang in that both are stereotyped manners of thought and expression. Clichés may be stampings from common speech, outworn phrases, or overworked quotations. Usually they express sound ideas (or ideas widely considered sound) and are memorably phrased. (If they were not sensible and stylistically appealing, they would never have been used so much as to become stale.) The problem with clichés is not that they are inexpressive but that they have been overused and misused to the point of weariness and ineffectiveness.

People with whom we often talk may bore us precisely because we know in advance what they are going to say and even the words and phrases they are going to use. In short, both what they say and how they say that something have become "molds" of thought and expression, constantly repeated. It should be kept in mind, too, that expressions which seem fresh and original to us may be clichés to those who have read and listened more than we have.

In daily speech, everyone is likely to use some clichés. When writing, you will discover that trite expressions leap to mind. Study of this list of trite expressions will help anyone to avoid hackneyed language and to strive for freshness and originality in both writing and speaking.

absence makes the heart grow
    fonder
acid test
add insult to injury
age before beauty
all boils down to
all in a lifetime
all in all
all is not gold that glitters
all sorts and conditions . . .
all things being equal
all wool and a yard wide
all work and no play
along this line
apple of one's eye
apple-pie order
arms of Morpheus
aroused our curiosity
as a matter of fact
as luck would have it
at one fell swoop
bark up the wrong tree
bated breath
bathed in tears
battle of life

beard the lion in his den
beat a hasty retreat
beating around the bush
beggars description
best bib and tucker
best foot forward
best-laid plans of mice and
    men
better late than never
better to have loved and lost
beyond the pale
bigger and better things
bitter end
blood is thicker than water
blow off steam
blow one's horn
blushing bride
blush of shame
bolt from the blue
born with a silver spoon
bosom of the family
brave as a lion
brawny arms
breathe a sigh of relief
bright and early

bright future
bright young countenance
bring home the bacon
brings to mind
briny deep
brown as a berry
budding genius
busy as a bee (beaver)
butterflies in (my) stomach
by leaps and bounds
caught red-handed
center of attraction
checkered career
cheer to the echo
cherchez la femme
chip off the old block
clear as mud
coals to Newcastle
cock and bull story
cold as ice
cold feet
cold sweat
come into the picture
common, or garden, variety
conspicuous by his (her) absence
consummation devoutly to be wished
cool as a cucumber
cradle of the deep
crow to pick
cut a long story short
cut the mustard
cynosure of all eyes
dainty repast
dead as a doornail
dead giveaway
deaf as a post

depths of despair
die is cast
distance lends enchantment
dog days
doomed to disappointment
down my alley
downy couch
draw the line
dreamy expression
drown one's sorrows
drunk as a skunk
duck (fish) out of water
dull thud
each and every
ear to the ground
eat, drink, and be merry
eat one's hat
epoch-making
et tu, Brute
exception proves the rule
eyes like stars
eyes of the world
face the music
fair sex
far cry
fast and loose
fat as a pig
fat's in the fire
favor with a selection
fearfully and wonderfully made
feather in his (her) cap
feathered choir
feel one's oats
festive board
few and far between
few well-chosen words
fight like a tiger

fill the bill
filthy lucre
fine and dandy
first and foremost
flash in the pan
flat as a pancake
flesh and blood
fly off the handle
fond farewell
fond memories
(a) fool and his money
fools rush in . . .
free as the air
fresh as a daisy
garden (common) variety
gentle as a lamb
get one's number
get the sack
get the upper hand
get up on the wrong side . . .
get what I mean?
gild the lily
give hostages to fortune
give it a try
glass of fashion
God's country
goes without saying
golden mean
(a) good time was had by all
goose hangs high
grain of salt
grand and glorious
graphic account (description)
greatness thrust upon . . .
green as grass
green with envy
Grim Reaper
grin like a Cheshire cat

hail fellow well met
hale and hearty
hand-to-mouth
hapless victim
happy as a lark
happy pair
hard row to hoe
haughty stare
haul over the coals
head over heels
heart of gold
heartless wretch
hew to the line
high on the hog
honest to goodness
hornet's nest (stir up)
hot as a pistol
hungry as a bear
if I had to do it over
if the truth be told
in a nutshell
inspiring sight
interesting to note
intestinal fortitude
in the last (final) analysis
in the long run
in this day and age
irons in the fire
irony of fate
it goes without saying
it stands to reason
jig is up
land-office business
last but not least
last straw
law unto himself (herself)
lead to the altar
lean and hungry look

lean over backward
leave in the lurch
leaves little to be desired
left-handed compliment
let one's hair down
let the cat out of the bag
lick into shape
like a blundering idiot
like a duck out of water
like a newborn babe
limp as a rag
little did I think
live it up
lock, stock, and barrel
mad as a wet hen
mad dash
main underlying reason
make a clean breast of
make ends meet
make hay while the sun shines
make night hideous
make no bones
make things hum
mantle of snow
many and varied
meets the eye
method in his madness
mind your *p*'s and *q*'s
missing the boat
monarch of all he (she) sur-
veys
moot question
more easily said than done
more than pleased
Mother Nature
motley crew (crowd)
must (a must)
naked truth

neat as a bandbox
necessary evil
needs no introduction
never a dull moment
nipped in the bud
no fooling
none the worse for wear
not to be sneezed at
not worth a Continental
number is up
of a high order
Old Sol
on the ball (stick)
open and shut
opportunity knocks but . . .
out of sight, out of mind
out of this world
over a barrel
ox in the ditch
parental rooftree
pay the piper (fiddler)
penny for your thoughts
pillar of society
pillar to post
play fast and loose
play second fiddle
play up to
point with pride
poor but honest
pretty as a picture
pretty kettle of fish
pretty penny
proud possessor
psychological moment
pull one's leg
pull the wool over . . .
pull up stakes
pure as the driven snow

put a bug (flea) in one's ear
put on the dog
rack one's brains
raining cats and dogs
read the riot act
red as a beet
rendered a selection
ring true
rub the wrong way
sad to relate
sadder but wiser
safe to say
sail under false colors
save for a rainy day
seal one's fate
seething mass
self-made man
sell like hot cakes
set one's cap for
set up shop
seventh heaven
show the white feather
shuffle off this mortal coil
sick and tired
sigh of relief
sight to behold
sing like a bird
sleep the sleep of the just
sow wild oats
start the ball rolling
steal one's thunder
stick in the craw
strong as an ox

stubborn as a mule
stuffed shirt
take it easy
tell it to the Marines
tenterhooks, be on
terra firma
that is to say
thing of the past
things like that
through thick and thin
throw in the sponge
throw the book at
time hangs heavy
tired as a dog
tired but happy
tit for tat
too funny for words
too many irons in the fire
top it off
trees like sentinels
truth to tell
turn over a new leaf
view with alarm
wee small hours
wet to the skin
where ignorance is bliss
wide open spaces
wild as a March hare
without further ado
wolf in sheep's clothing
wunderbar
you can say that again
your guess is as good as mine

Make Sentences Complete

We think in words and speak and write in sentences. Such a statement is not entirely true, but it implies that by the use of words we phrase sentences that are tied together to make up a complete piece of writing. A sentence is the link—the only link—between a thought and full development of that thought. Like all links, it is of great importance.

If one's sentences are awkward, vague, or faulty, the primary purpose of writing has been defeated at the outset. A major step to better writing is finding out what a sentence is and discovering what faults in structure and function are most likely to keep it from being complete, clear, direct, and communicative. Because sentences are so important, this seventh step and the next six are devoted to their characteristics and their flaws.

THE GRAMMAR OF SENTENCES

A usable definition of a sentence is that it is "one or more words conveying to the reader a sense of complete meaning." The word (or group of words) normally, but not always, has a subject and predicate. The subject may be expressed or it may be understood and not expressed. Either subject or predicate may be understood from the context.

Remember that the foregoing statements refer to *grammatical* completeness. In one sense we do not have a complete thought until we have read or written a series of sentences. A pronoun in one sentence may take its meaning from an antecedent in another. Such words as *thus, these, another,* and *again,* and such phrases as *for example* and *on the other hand* frequently show that the thought about to be presented in a new sentence is related to the thought in a preceding sentence or paragraph.

When we say, then, that a sentence conveys a "sense of complete meaning" to the reader, we do not imply that we can dispense with its context (the statements which precede or follow it). We mean only that we have a group of words so ordered as to be *grammatically* self-sufficient. For example, the statement, "He took command on July 3, 1775," is grammatically complete. It has a subject, the pronoun *he,* and it has a verb, *took* (took command). In this sense the entire statement is complete and must be begun with a capital letter and be followed by a period. So far as total meaning is concerned, however, we need other sentences to tell us that *he* refers to George Washington and that the command which he assumed was that of Continental Forces in the War of the American Revolution.

The study of grammar may be of little value in itself. To be able to say by rote "A sentence is a group of words containing a single, complete thought, or a group of closely related thoughts" is valueless in writing or speaking grammatically correct sentences unless the terms of the definition are understood, unless comprehension of the functions of parts of speech, of various kinds of sentences, gives meaning to that definition. To learn the parts of speech, to distinguish simple, complex, and compound sentences—such additions to our knowledge represent wasted effort until we see such knowledge operating upon the sentences which we write or speak. We will then see why the study of grammar is of little value in itself, but we will see more than that—we will find ourselves writing sentences grammatically correct and will know *why* and *how* we do so.

To learn to phrase good sentences, basic units of thought, is a worthwhile achievement. It has been said that the simple declarative sentence is the greatest achievement of the human intellect.

SENTENCE INCOMPLETENESS

Henry David Thoreau once wrote "A sentence should read as if its author, had he held a plough instead of a pen, could have drawn a furrow deep and straight to the end." In writing, it is all too easy to begin a sentence well enough but to waver, pause, go off the path, and fail to complete what has been started.

The word *sentence* can mean "a stated opinion." By this definition, all words, or groups of words, which "make sense" to your reader or listener can be called sentences. But remember these two requirements for a *complete* sentence: (1) it must have both a subject and a predicate (verb) which actually appear or are clearly implied (understood); (2) it must not begin with a connecting word such as *although*, *as*, *because*, *before*, and *while* unless an independent clause follows immediately in the same construction.

This is a complete sentence: "Dick has bought a new jacket." Omit *Dick* (subject) or *has bought* (verb) and not enough remains to make a full sentence. Also, substituting for *has bought* a compound participle such as *having bought* produces an incomplete statement: "Dick having bought a new jacket." If a word such as *although* precedes *Dick*, the sentence is incomplete for another reason: the clause, "Although Dick has bought a new jacket," expresses an idea, but it depends on some other statement and is not capable of standing alone. If you don't like Dick, you might write: "Although Dick has bought a new jacket, he still looks like a hayseed."

1. A phrase is not a sentence

A phrase is only part of a full sentence. It should be attached to, or should be expressed within, the sentence of which it is a part. Or the phrase should be made complete in itself by adding what is needed, usually a subject, or verb, or both.

Incorrect   *Winter being mild last year*. I had to start mowing the lawn weeks earlier than usual.

Correct   *Winter being mild last year,* I had to start mowing the lawn weeks earlier than usual.

Winter was mild last year, and I had to start mowing the lawn weeks earlier than usual.

2. A dependent clause is not a sentence

Adverbial and adjective clauses can never stand alone; they always *depend* upon something else for completeness. Correcting a dependent clause fragment often involves no change in wording; sometimes, changing a capital to a small letter and a period to a comma or to no mark at all will correct the error. Sometimes, you may prefer to make a dependent adverbial clause into an independent clause by omitting a subordinating conjunction and make an independent clause of an adjective clause by changing the relative pronoun to a personal one.

Incorrect: I had no money for the trip. *When suddenly Jack paid me what he had borrowed.* (Adverbial)

Sue lived in Akron for five years. *From which her family moved to Atlanta.* (Adjective)

Correct: I had no money for the trip. Suddenly Jack paid me what he had borrowed.

Sue lived in Akron for five years, from which her family moved to Atlanta.

3. Avoid starting a sentence with one construction and then stopping or shifting to another

An unfinished or incomplete sentence results when a writer begins a statement and then shifts his thought and construction, keeps adding words, yet stops before he has given meaning to his opening words. Or the writer may start with an independent clause but then add an unfinished statement which he forgets to coordinate with his first independent statement. In correcting such unfinished constructions, the writer should determine carefully what is missing and then supply it, in proper grammatical elements:

Incomplete: An old woman in the apartment, who, because she had become progressively more lame, was forced to use a cane and then to be confined to a wheelchair.

Improved: An old woman in the apartment, who, because she had become progressively more lame, was forced to use a cane and then to be confined to a wheelchair, ordered the landlord to install a telephone in her kitchen.

Incomplete: I thought that preparing dinner for eight guests would be a simple matter, but after deciding on a menu and shopping for the food, being very careful to stay within my budget, and then spending hours over a hot stove that burned the lima beans and three of my fingers.

Improved: I thought that preparing dinner for eight guests would be a simple matter, but after deciding on a menu and shopping for the food, being very careful to stay within my budget, and then spending hours over a hot stove that burned the lima beans and three of my fingers, I realized that a dinner party is a formidable undertaking.

Now you know that a major fault in sentence structure is incompleteness. And yet it should be noted that some statements convey a full thought without employing an actual or implied subject or verb. Such expressions as *Hello, Good-by, Of course, But to continue,* and *Never again* make clear statements. Sentence fragments appear in stories, novels, and plays because they reflect normal conversation. But in writing sentences, remember that none is complete unless it fully and clearly transmits to your reader a complete thought or closely knit group of thoughts.

Punctuate Sentences Correctly

As you already know, and as is pointed out in Step 17, every sentence should end with a period, question mark, or exclamation point. But that is not the entire problem. You not only should make certain that sentences punctuated as sentences are complete (Step 7), but that they appear one at a time.

When thoughts stray from or dart ahead of writing, you may find that, instead of setting down full sentences one at a time, you are joining, or splicing, with a comma statements which should be separated by a period or should be linked by a semicolon, a colon, or a conjunction *and* a comma. Such comma splices, considered faulty in both punctuation and in sentence construction, are serious flaws because the reader cannot determine where one sentence ends and the next one begins.

An even more serious error than the comma splice is the fused sentence; in the former at least some indication of separation between statements is given, in the latter two complete sentences are fused or pushed together with no punctuation at all. The reader is therefore unable to distinguish where one full thought ends and another begins.

THE COMMA SPLICE

Comma splices, or "comma faults," occur in several forms:

1. Two statements which are not grammatically related but which are related by content.

2. Two related statements, the second of which begins with a personal pronoun whose antecedent is in the first.
3. Two related statements, the second of which begins with a demonstrative pronoun or adjective (*that, this, those, these, such*).
4. Two statements, the second of which contains, or begins with, a conjunctive adverb (*however, then*, and so on).

In order of the faults given above, consider these comma splices:

A meeting of the committee is scheduled for tonight, many important items are on the agenda.

The physician examined the patient carefully, he did not say a word.

Drive carefully when you near the bridge, this is very narrow.

I was late for the lecture, however, Mr. James did not scold me.

The comma splice error can be corrected in several ways:

1. Use a period after the first statement and a capital letter at the beginning of the second.
2. Use a semicolon between the statements.
3. Subordinate one of the statements and retain the comma.
4. Insert a conjunction between statements, or as a substitute for the conjunctive adverb, and retain the comma.

Each of the comma splices illustrated above can be corrected in more than one of the four ways shown. For instance, the first "sentence" may be revised as follows:

A meeting of the committee is scheduled for tonight. Many important items are on the agenda.

A meeting of the committee is scheduled for tonight; many important items are on the agenda.

A meeting of the committee has been scheduled for tonight, and many important items are on the agenda.

In rewriting "comma splice sentences," be careful to avoid a series of short, choppy sentences. Also, do not try to show a causal (cause and effect) relationship where in fact it does not really exist.

An occasional comma splice can be both suitable and stylistically valid. Many writers and professional editors carefully avoid all comma splices of whatever kind, but a case can be made for using a comma in such constructions as these:

> I worked, I struggled, I failed.
> That is Alice, this is Betty.
> We are not going to the library, we are going to a movie.

THE FUSED SENTENCE

A fused sentence is one in which two independent and distinct statements are "blended." That is, separate statements are run together with no mark of punctuation between them or a comma is used when a stronger mark is indicated. Consider these two sentences:

> The Depression deepened its hold on American business thousands of men lost their jobs and breadlines became a common sight.
> When he left the Army, Herbert took up horseracing this activity is often called the Sport of Kings.

Judged by grammatical standards, each of these "sentences" contains two independent and distinct statements which can be written separately. If the writer decides that the two statements are sufficiently related in thought, he may choose to connect them more closely with punctuation which is not terminal.

> The Depression deepened its hold on American business. Thousands of men lost their jobs and breadlines became a common sight.
> When he left the Army, Herbert took up horseracing. This activity is often called the Sport of Kings.
> When he left the Army, Herbert took up horseracing, often called the Sport of Kings.

In correcting a fused sentence, do not fall into the trap of the comma splice. Use of a comma may be a less grave error than using no punctuation at all, but that is debatable. Note this sentence:

We lived in Madison two years ago, our house was in the center of town.

Using a comma after *ago* is incorrect. One of the four methods by which a comma splice may be corrected should be applied to the correction of a fused sentence:

We lived in Madison two years ago. Our house was in the center of town.

We lived in Madison two years ago; our house was in the center of town.

We lived in Madison two years ago, and our house was in the center of town.

When we lived in Madison two years ago, our house was in the center of town.

STEP NINE

Put Words
in Order

Some languages are highly inflected. That is, the endings of nouns, adjectives, adverbs, and verbs in such languages are varied and it is easy to identify their relationships to each other and to other words in a sentence. The English language is not highly inflected. Words in an English sentence have meaning largely because of their position: they mean one thing in one position, another in another, and have little meaning at all in still another position. Many experts contend that the true basis of English grammar is word order.

Note how the meaning of "My *first* husband's job was in market research" changes when the position of *first* is shifted: "My husband's *first* job was in market research." "I was invited to a party *tonight*" has a meaning different from that of "I was *tonight* invited to a party."

Step Nine suggests that (1) related words should be kept together; (2) words should not be misplaced and allowed to dangle; (3) words that belong together should not be needlessly separated.

MISPLACED MODIFIERS

A word that describes, limits, or "modifies" another word should be so placed that the relationship between the two is unmistakable. When a modifier is placed so that it could as readily modify the word or phrase preceding it as the word or phrase immediately following, it is said to "look two ways" or to be a "squinting" modifier. In the sentence "The boy who is delivering our newspaper *currently* needs a haircut," there is ambiguity: is the boy who needs a haircut in current possession of the delivery chore, or is the official delivery boy in current tonsorial distress?

To clear up the confusion, you should revise. One way to do this is to add *certainly* after *currently*. In this way, you indicate that the adverb *currently* modifies *is delivering*, and the adverb *certainly* applies to *needs*. Another method is to move the modifier and include it with the material it modifies, i.e., transfer *currently* to a position between *who* and *is*, or (if such is the writer's intention) to a position following *haircut*. If the resulting sentence is still awkward, rewrite it.

Or consider this sentence: The person who can do this *well* deserves praise. *Well* may modify either *can do* or *deserves*. You should revise. One way to clear up the confusion is to add *certainly* after *well*. Now the adverb *well* modifies *can do*, and the adverb *certainly* applies to *deserves*.

Take another example: The repairman who does his work quietly *from the point of view of the housewife* is worthy of praise. The "squinting" italicized phrases should appear at the beginning or end of the sentence, which will still be wordy and awkward but at least understandable.

Words such as *only*, *even*, *hardly*, *not*, and *scarcely* require careful placing. They are associated with the word or phrase immediately following or immediately preceding. In the sentence "He *hardly* has enough money for the purchase," *hardly* may be thought to modify "has"; actually, it is probably intended to modify "enough." To remove any possible doubt, revise the sentence to read "He has *hardly* enough money for the purchase."

Here is a sentence containing eleven words: *Only the foreman told me to finish the job before noon*. In it the word *only* can appear in every position from one through eleven: The *only* foreman told me . . ., the foreman *only* told me . . ., the foreman told *only* me . . ., and so on. The position of *only* will provide eleven somewhat different meanings for the sentence. (Note that placing it in the sixth position causes a split infinitive, perhaps not a very sound idea.)

The position of phrases and clauses can also provide confusion. It is not likely that writers of the following expressed what they meant to say:

Last month the Capitol was closed for alterations to all visitors. (*To all visitors* should appear after *closed*; the resulting sentence will be no gem, but at least confusion will disappear.)

The preacher discussed everyday affairs and people whom you and I know *as simply as a little child*. (Place the italicized phrase after *discussed* or at the beginning of the sentence.)

DANGLING MODIFIERS

Any misplaced word, phrase, or clause dangles in the sense that it hangs loosely within a sentence. The word another word or group of words is intended to modify should never be taken for granted; it should be expressed and it should be placed so that your readers can easily make the intended association.

The term *dangling* applies especially to verbal phrases and elliptical clauses, the correct position of which depends upon logical, careful thinking.

Sentences containing dangling verbal phrases may be corrected in three ways: (1) by expanding the verbal phrase to a dependent clause; (2) by supplying the substantive (noun or pronoun) that the dangling phrase *should* modify; (3) by placing the construction so near the supplied substantive that no confusion is possible.

Incorrect: *Walking down the aisle*, the curtain rose. (Participial phrase)

To play tennis well, a good racquet is needed. (Infinitive phrase)

By exercising every day, your health will improve. (Gerund phrase)

Correct: While we were walking down the aisle, the curtain rose.

Walking down the aisle, John saw the curtain rise.

We, walking down the aisle, saw the curtain rise.

(This revision is no great improvement because it widely separates subject and verb.)

The two other incorrect sentences given may also be improved by one of the three methods suggested. Most of us don't mind making an error, but we do dislike being thought incoherent or ludicrous, both of which these sentences definitely are.

When a verbal phrase is used to denote a general action rather than a specific one, it is *not* considered a dangling modifier: *Considering everything*, his suggestion was reasonable.

Dangling elliptical clauses create a related problem. *Ellipsis* means "an omission," "something left out." An elliptical clause is one without a subject, or verb, or both; it dangles unless the implied (understood) subject is the same as that of the main clause.

Incorrect: *When 19 years old*, my grandfather died.

While working last night, the lights went out.

Before thoroughly warmed up, you should not race a motor.

To correct such confused sentences, insert in the dangling clause the needed subject and verb, or change the subject (or subject and verb) in the main clause.

When I was 19 years old, my grandfather died.

When 19 years old, I grieved because my grandfather had died.

While I was working last night, the lights went out.

Before it is thoroughly warmed up, you should not race a motor.

You should thoroughly warm up a motor before you race it.

SPLIT CONSTRUCTIONS

Separating, or splitting, closely related parts of a sentence is not always incorrect. But splitting verbs in a verb phrase, the two parts of an infinitive, and a preposition and its object often results in awkwardness and lack of clarity. Whenever possible, keep logically related elements together.

Split infinitive

When a word, phrase, or clause comes between the sign of the infinitive, *to*, and a verb, the construction is called a *split infinitive*. Reputable speakers and writers occasionally split an infinitive; consequently, this error is no longer considered as grave as it once was. Also, on rare occasions, you must split an infinitive to make clear and exact what you have in mind. For example, in this sentence, "Martha wants *to really see* Tod in person," moving *really* to any other place in the sentence would change the meaning or weaken the effectiveness of the sentence.

Normally, however, no sound reason exists for putting an adverb or phrase or other group of words between *to* and a verb. "He requested us to *as soon as possible* leave the building" would be clearer and more natural if the italicized words were moved to the end of the sentence.

Separating the parts of a verb phrase

Splitting an auxiliary verb and a main verb is rarely effective or natural. Consider the following sentences:

> The speaker *has*, although one would hardly believe it, *been* lecturing for over an hour.
> This was the recording we *had* before we left Chicago *heard* so often in discotheques.
> He *has*, to my great surprise, *sung* very well.

By bringing together the words in italics, the sentences become more clear and direct:

Although one would hardly believe it, the speaker *has been* lecturing for over an hour.

This was the recording we *had heard* so often in discotheques before we left Chicago.

To my great surprise, he *has sung* very well.

Subject and verb, preposition and object

Separation of such elements is occasionally justifiable. But in awkward and generally ineffective sentences like the following, the italicized elements should be brought together:

Jack, as soon as he heard the question, *raised his hand.* (Subject and verb)

Mabel crept *into*, although she was terrified, *the frail canoe.* (Preposition and object)

Mary *asked*, even before I could finish, *what I really meant.* (Subject and object)

Coordinate elements

Two coordinate phrases or two coordinate dependent clauses should not be widely separated. Because of their approximately equal weight, they should be brought together and their relationship indicated by the appropriate coordinating conjunction:

Ineffective: *Although he was conscientious on the job*, he could not win a promotion, *although he performed many extra duties.*

Effective: *Although he was conscientious on the job* and *although he performed many extra duties*, he could not win a promotion.

Ineffective: *Unless the blizzard lets up*, we cannot make it to the mountain lodge, *unless the roads are passable.*

Effective: *Unless the blizzard lets up*, and *unless the roads are passable*, we cannot make it to the mountain lodge.

STEP TEN

Make Sentences Logical

Seeing to it that sentences are complete, properly punctuated, and with their words in order constitute three major steps toward better writing. Unfortunately, that is still not enough. Because we don't always think, or think carefully, we can and do construct sentences that violate common sense and logic. Our minds are often inadequate, but they are all we have for thinking. Nowhere more than in writing sentences do we need to use them.

You can expect your reader to give careful attention, but you should not expect him to untangle mixed and involved constructions or to correct your mistakes in thinking.

An illogical construction involves a grouping of words that (1) is contrary to reason, (2) violates some principle of regularity, (3) fails to make good sense, (4) omits an important word or words, (5) adds an element which has no grammatical function, (6) substitutes a dependent clause functioning as one part of speech for another.

These six kinds of mixed and illogical structures can be examined under several headings.

1. Omission of a necessary verb

In both speaking and writing, we often omit words without necessarily being illogical or unclear. "He always has worked hard and always will [work hard]" is understandable without the bracketed words. But it is doubtful that the following sentence could be considered complete: The floor is swept and the dishes washed. In this sentence, *is* is understood to accompany *washed*. But *dishes is washed* is wrong. We should write: The floor is swept and the dishes *are* washed.

I never have and probably never will write good letters. (The word *written* should be added after *have*.)

2. Omission of other essential words

If a necessary article, pronoun, conjunction, or preposition is omitted, your meaning will not be clear or, worse, may be misinterpreted.

> The Chairman and Chief Executive received us. (This sentence may mean that one person is both Chairman and Chief Executive. If you mean to indicate two people, add *the* after *and*.)
>
> I have interest and regard for your work. (Add *in* after *interest*.)
>
> She asked that question be repeated. (Add another *that* before *question*.)

3. Omission of words in a comparison

Doubtful: He is so wealthy.
            Your report was the greatest success.
            His feet are bigger than any boy in town.
Clearer: He is so wealthy that he never needs to think about money.
            Your report was the greatest success of any received thus far.
            His feet are bigger than those of any other boy in town.

4. Mixed or double comparison

A confused construction may occur when you try to include two comparisons in the same statement. Good usage permits a double comparison in the same sentence but only when the second appears after the first has been completed.

Illogical: The Battle of Stalingrad was *one of the greatest if not the greatest* single conflict of all time.

Preferable: The Battle of Stalingrad was *one of the greatest single conflicts of all time, if not the greatest.*

5. *Confusing blends*

Certain blends may creep into anyone's writing. *Regardless* and *irrespective* are good words but are often faultily blended into *irregardless*. *In spite of* and *despite* may be illogically blended into *despite of*: *Despite of* what you say, I am not convinced. Blending *where* (meaning *at* or *in which*) with *at which* results in expressions such as "*Where* does she live *at*?" and "The town *where* I live *in.*"

6. *Double negatives*

Everyday speech is filled with expressions such as "haven't scarcely" and "can't help but." These are forms of what is called the *double negative*, two negative terms in the same statement. The double negative was used repeatedly by Chaucer, Shakespeare, and many other great writers of the past. It still appears regularly in correct French. Double negatives in English today, however, are considered out of style and unacceptable.

You are not likely to write, or often hear, such expressions as "I didn't see nobody" and "I didn't get none." You should avoid such commonly used and less obviously illiterate expressions as "I did *not* have *but* two," "one *can't* help *but*," "*not scarcely* enough," and "*not hardly* any."

7. *Misuse of dependent clauses*

Dependent clauses function as parts of speech; to substitute an adverbial clause for a noun clause is as illogical as to use an adverb in place of a noun.

Dubious: *Because she had no new dress* was the reason Joy stayed at home.

Eleanor noted *where the paper says* that it will snow tonight.

Correct: Joy stayed at home *because she had no new dress.*

That she had no new dress was the reason Joy stayed at home.

> Eleanor noted *that the paper says* it will snow tonight.

Using an adverbial clause in place of a noun or noun phrase is as illogical as using it for a noun clause. *When*, *where*, and *because* clauses are chief offenders in this form of illogicality:

Dubious: Stealing *is when (is where)* one takes the property of another without permission and with stealth.

                My high fever was *because* I was in a weak condition.

Clear: Stealing is taking the property of another without permission and with stealth.

                Stealing is the act of taking the property . . .

                My weak condition caused my high fever.

                That I was in a weak condition was the cause . . .

A noun clause, not a complete sentence, should be the subject or object or complement of *is* and *was*. A quotation may be the subject or complement of *is* and *was*: "When I have fears that I may cease to be" is a line from Keats' famous poem. Ordinarily, however, you should convert a sentence into a noun clause (or, rarely, a noun phrase) in this construction.

Illogical: I had lost my nerve was the reason I did not try.

                Fred's only hope is he will get his paycheck today.

Improved: The reason that I did not try was that I had lost my nerve.

                Fred's only hope is that he will get his paycheck today.

                Fred has only one hope: getting his paycheck today.

STEP ELEVEN

Make Sentence Structure Consistent

Consistency in a sentence means that its various parts are similar and in agreement and should remain so unless there is good reason for shifting them. Step Eleven consists of avoiding shifts in tense, subject and voice, number, class or person of pronouns, figures of speech, and mood. Keeping all these elements consistent is not difficult but does require a little thought and care.

Be consistent in tense

Tense indicates the time of a verb (past, present, future). A careless writer is likely to shift from past to present time or from present to past or back and forth between the two. Consider this sentence:

> Jill *was walking* briskly along the sidewalk when suddenly a Honda *turned* the corner. It *careens* wildly down the street, twisting as if its rider *is* unconscious. Jill *leaped* to one side.

The writer began with the past tense: *was walking* and *turned*. He then shifted to the present tense: *careens* and *is*. Finally, he reverted to the past tense: *leaped*. To be consistent (that is, avoid shifts in tense), *careens* should be *careened* and *is* should be *were* or *was*. Or, of course, the entire sentence could be put into the present, in which case it would start with *is walking* and never shift to the past.

Be consistent in subject and voice

Voice is a term in grammar which indicates whether the subject is acting (active) or being acted upon (passive). In general, the active voice is more effective than the passive; however, adhering to the use of either one removes a major cause of shifts in subject. Ordinarily, one should have a single subject in a sentence and should use only one voice.

Faulty: The diesel engine burns little kerosene, and Ed says it is completely reliable.

As you sail across the harbor, channel markers can be seen.

Improved: Ed says that the diesel engine burns little kerosene and is completely reliable.

As you sail across the harbor, you can see channel markers.

Be consistent in the use of number

Frequent mistakes in the use of number are careless switchings from plural nouns to singular nouns, or singular to plural, or failing to make pronouns agree in number with their antecedents.

Faulty: I enjoy an ice cream soda, but *they* tend to make me fat.

If men really try their best, *he is* bound to succeed.

If boys treated Grandmother with respect, she would surely respect *him*.

Improved: I enjoy an ice cream soda, but *it* tends to make me fat.

If men really try their best, *they are* bound to succeed.

If boys treated Grandmother with respect, she would surely respect *them*.

Avoid shifting the class or person of pronouns

A shift in pronoun reference violates the rule that pronouns and antecedents must agree in person. The most common occurrence of this fault is shifting from the third person to the second.

> If *one* tries hard enough, *you* will usually succeed. (*One* is an indefinite pronoun in the third person; *you* is a personal pronoun in the second person. The sentence should read: "If *you* try hard enough, *you*. . . ." or "If *one* tries hard enough, *he*. . . .")

Be consistent in using figures of speech

Figures of speech, that is, words used not in their literal sense but for the images they suggest, are occasionally effective and vivid. However, guard against sudden switches from literal to figurative speech and switches from one figure to another:

> That foreman is a cold fish who always has an axe to grind.

Before we pass judgment on the foreman, we must answer a question: what use has a fish for an axe? This is a clearer statement:

> That disdainful foreman always has a selfish motive.

Be consistent in the use of mood

Mood (sometimes spelled *mode*) is a grammatical term indicating the style or fashion of a verb. Mood suggests the state of mind or the manner in which a statement is made: a fact, a request, a command, a probability, a condition. English has three moods, *indicative* (He *has come* to see us); *imperative* (*Come* here at once); and *subjunctive* (Suppose he *were* to come).

Do not needlessly shift from indicative to imperative or subjunctive or mix their use. The sentence "Last spring I *would play* tennis every morning and *swam* every afternoon" should read "Last spring I *would play* tennis every morning and *would swim* every afternoon" or "Last spring I *played* tennis every morning and *swam* every afternoon."

Make Sentences Unified

Unity means "oneness," "singleness of purpose," "being united or combined as one." In writing, unity implies that every sentence should contain a single thought or a group of closely related thoughts. Making sentences unified is an aid in keeping the writer settled on the track and the reader focused on what is being conveyed to him.

Unity has little to do with length; a long sentence may be unified and a short one ununified. This long sentence forms a unit of thought: Although Lee liked her fellow employees, especially Mary Ellen and Harvey, she was tired of working and decided to resign and marry Henry. But this short sentence lacks unity: Mary Ellen was a good worker, and she had a friend named Henry.

Sentence unity is violated in two principal ways: (1) putting too many details into one sentence and (2) placing unrelated ideas together.

Rambling sentences with too many details

Here are two rambling sentences containing excessive detail. Each has been rewritten to indicate how such sentences can be made more unified:

> Faulty: He was reared in Southport, a village in Connecticut, which has only about 1,000 inhabitants, but which has a famous yacht club,

three churches, an excellent public library, several tree-lined residential streets, and a good motel, being located just off U.S. Highway 95.

As I grew older, my desire to play basketball grew also, and when I entered high school I was too small to play my first two years of school, being only five feet tall, so I had to sit on the bench, but later in high school I began to grow, and before I graduated my senior year I was playing center on the first team, for I had grown 13 inches in two years.

Improved: He was reared in Southport, Connecticut, a village of about 1,000 inhabitants which is located just off U.S. Highway 95. Southport has several tree-lined residential streets, an excellent public library, a motel, three churches, and a famous yacht club.

Although my interest in basketball had grown with the years, I discovered upon entering high school that my physical growth had not kept pace with my desire to play. For two years my five-foot frame glumly occupied the bench. That before I graduated I was playing center on the first team I contend is due to a genuine, if familiar, miracle: in the years between I had grown 13 inches.

Unrelated ideas in the same sentence

You can achieve unity in a sentence containing unrelated ideas by showing some evidence of relationship or by subordinating one idea. If the ideas are not closely related and relationship cannot logically be indicated, place them in separate sentences: If no relationship whatever is evident, omit one of the ideas.

Faulty: His brother was a tall man, and he was a good fisherman.

Improved: His brother, a tall man who loved the sea, was a good fisherman.

His brother was a tall man. He was also a good fisherman.

Make Sentences Concise

Nearly everyone uses more words than he needs. This overuse is especially noticeable in conversation, but many written sentences are guilty of the same fault. Careful attention to sentence structure will usually result in a wholesale removal of words that add little or nothing to meaning or effectiveness.

Much of the most memorable writing the world has ever known is short, sharp, and word-hungry: The Golden Rule is eleven words long. The Ten Commandments are given in only seventy-five words. The most notable speech ever delivered on this continent, Lincoln's Gettysburg Address, consists of two hundred and twenty-seven words.

WORDY PHRASES AND EXPRESSIONS

It is a sound rule never to use two words where one will do or twenty words where ten will serve. It is more effective to refer to "the chance of war" than to say (as has been said by a noted writer) "in the regrettable eventuality of a failure of the deterrence policy." A speaker was once asked whether certain rules should be observed. He could have said "yes." Instead he replied "The implementation of sanctions will inevitably eventuate in repercussions." A recent governmental pamphlet contained this monstrous sentence: "Endemic insect populations cause little-realized amounts of damage to forage and timber." What did the writer mean? Probably "Native insects harm trees and grass more than we realize."

Such writing is of course gobbledygook: inflated, pompous, and wordy. You may never be guilty of writing such highflown sentences as these, but it is likely that your work does contain numerous wordy expressions. Study the following list and check your own sentences to see how many of them appear:

Reduce These	**To These**
a certain length of time	a certain time
advance planning	planning
after the conclusion of	after
as a result of	because
at the present time	now
at this point in time	now
before long	soon
by means of	by
by the time	when
come in contact with	meet
due to the fact that	since (due to)
during the time that	while
for the amount of	for
get in touch with	telephone (write, meet)
hurry up	hurry
in accordance with	by
inasmuch as	since
in case	if
in connection with	with
in lieu of	instead
in order to	to
in regard to	about
in the event that	if
in the month of April	in April
in this day and age	today
in view of the fact that	since
it has come to our attention that	(begin with the word following *that*)
it is interesting to note that	(begin with the word following *that*)
I would appreciate it if	please

Reduce These	To These
of an indefinite nature	indefinite
of great importance	important
on condition that	if
provided that	if
under date of May 5	of May 5
with the exception of	except

The foregoing list is only a sampling of hundreds of wordy expressions that could be named. Comb sentences carefully to see what can be eliminated without real loss. For example, you will find that "there is" and "there are" sentences are customarily wordy: "In this building there are five elevators that await inspection" can do quite well without "there are" and "that." Cutting out unnecessary words can become an interesting game, a game that will increase the effectiveness of your writing.

As a further aid in detecting wordiness, study this additional list of wordy expressions:

absolutely essential
around about that time
audible to the ear
back up
bisect in two
call up on the 'phone
choose up
Christmas Eve evening
combine together
complete monopoly
completely unanimous
connect up with
consensus of opinion
cooperate together
cover over
descend down
each and everyone

endorse on the back
entirely eliminated
extreme prime importance
few (many) in number
final end (outcome)
first beginnings
four-cornered square
from whence
important essentials
individual person
join together
long length
loquacious talker
many in number
meet up with
more angrier
more better

more older

more paramount

more perfect

more perpendicular

most unique

most unkindest

necessary essential

necessary need

old adage

personal friend

recur again

reduce down

repeat again

resume again

return back

revert back to

rise up

round in form

separate out

(a) short half-hour

small in size

sunset in the west

talented genius

this afternoon at 4 P.M.

this morning at 8 A.M.

visible to the eye

REDUCING PREDICATION

Reducing predication means decreasing the number of words used to make a statement. Consider these suggestions:

1. Combine two short sentences into one.
    From: He was a mechanic in a repair shop. He specialized in carburetor adjustment.
    To: He was a garage mechanic, specializing in carburetor adjustment.

2. Reduce a compound or complex sentence to a simple sentence.
    From: Sarah Bernhardt was for many years an excellent actress, and everyone admired her talent.

    Everyone admired the talent of Sarah Bernhardt, who was for many years an excellent actress.
    To: Everyone admired the talent of Sarah Bernhardt, for years an excellent actress.

3. Reduce a clause to a phrase.
    From: a haze that resembled the color of smoke
    To: a haze the color of smoke

4. Reduce a phrase to a single word.
   From: a haze the color of smoke
   To: a smoke-colored haze
5. Reduce two or more words to one.
   From: a foreman in the Department of Shipping
   To: a shipping foreman

UNNECESSARY DETAILS

Using unnecessary details is known as *prolixity*. A prolix
sentence obscures or weakens the main idea.

Wordy: Last winter the squash tournament was won by
               Barry Stebbins with a racquet he had pur-
               chased two months before from a friend of
               his who had bought a new one made of cat-
               gut and who sold Barry his old one for $8.50.
Improved: Last winter the squash tournament was won by
               Barry Stebbins with a racquet he had bought
               from a friend for $8.50.
Still better: Last winter Barry Stebbins won the squash
               tournament with a second-hand racquet.

USELESS REPETITION

The needless repetition of an idea without providing additional force or clearness is called *tautology*. This flaw is obvious
in the following sentence: This entirely new and novel in-
novation in our program will delight our TV viewing audience;
it has just been introduced for the first time and will cause
pleasure to many people who will be watching.

Faulty: Peggy was anxious for Jack to succeed and eager
               that he do so.
               In all necessary essentials the work is com-
               pleted and finished.
Improved: Peggy was eager for Jack to succeed.
               In all essentials the work is completed.

Brevity has been called the "soul of wit." It is more than that: it is an indispensable aid in writing effective sentences. Using no unnecessary words is hardly an attainable goal by anyone, but eliminating most useless, space-consuming, time-wasting words and expressions constitutes a major step toward better writing.

STEP FOURTEEN

Develop Paragraphs Fully and Interestingly

When you write, you become a builder engaged in a construction process. You build letters into words, words into sentences, and sentences into paragraphs. Only a jerry-built house results from flimsy materials; only a jerry-built piece of writing will result from poor diction, flabby sentences, and inept paragraphs.

A paragraph is a group of related sentences, a logical unit developing one thought or a part of one thought. It is a bundle, or sequence, of sentences tied together for the convenience of readers: a visual unit.

Good paragraphing is a real aid to clarity. Properly separated groups of sentences let the writer plot his course and see the progress he is making. They serve the reader by making the structure and development of ideas apparent. Paragraphing involves some of the principles of punctuation in that it separates certain ideas from others because of their structural relationships; it furnishes the reader signposts to guide him along the writer's paths of thought.

The sentence is the unit of writing, but the paragraph is the unit of developed thought. In fact, the heart of learning to write effectively is found in paragraph development. The secret of the effective writer—if he may be said to have a secret—is his ability to form a thought, however fragmentary or vague, and then to develop it so that it is clear, helpful, and interesting to readers.

Hasn't everyone had the experience of making a statement or writing a sentence and then halting, aware that it needs expansion, certain that the one idea standing alone seems bare and incomplete, but not knowing what to say or write to "flesh it out"? This problem is the core of the writing process.

Suppose, for example, the thought occurs to you, as well it might, that "the calendar is a foolish invention." But this idea obviously needs further comment. Can you explain what you mean? Add a thought or two to it? Build it into a paragraph? After some thought, you may be able to write this much:

> The calendar is a foolish invention. It tells us that the new year begins in winter. But everyone knows that school and business start afresh in the autumn, and nature has its re-birth in spring.

This is still an only partly clothed idea, but it has a little something to wear.

Like everything else in the process of writing, effective paragraphs depend upon effective thinking. One must train his mind to deal fully and logically with an idea, or series of ideas, to develop concepts and relate them to each other.

Good paragraphs have four major characteristics:

1. A central idea and purpose
2. Adequate development
3. Proper proportion and length
4. Absence of any unrelated material

Topic sentences

Every paragraph should have a central idea and purpose expressed or implied in a topic (or thesis) sentence. The topic sentence is the statement in a paragraph that tells the reader which topic or which aspect of a larger topic the paragraph is intended to develop. It states, suggests, or in some other way indicates the heart, the core, of the idea which is to be, is being, or has been developed.

Generally, the topic sentence comes first. Occasionally, it may appear somewhere toward the middle or at the end of the paragraph, depending upon content and the writer's method of organizing it. Sometimes the topic sentence is not expressed at all but is implied by the paragraph as a whole.

When you begin a paragraph with a topic sentence, you make a definite commitment on what you are about to discuss and you arouse the reader's expectation. If your paragraph is successful, it will fulfill the promise in your initial sentence and satisfy the reader. Consider how the following paragraph achieves both objectives. The topic sentence is shown in italics.

With his telescope Galileo made some important astronomical discoveries. For instance, he discovered that there are satellites around the planet Jupiter. He saw that the moon was not flat, as people commonly believed, but that it had high and low areas, and he even calculated the height of some of its mountains. The Milky Way revealed itself to him as a vast collection of stars, and by studying sunspots he reached the conclusion that the sun rotates.

Each paragraph you write can begin with a topic sentence, but to avoid monotony, you can occasionally change the position of topic sentences. Note that in the following, the topic sentence, placed at the end, sums up the thought rather than introducing it:

Galileo was the first man to discover that there are satellites around the planet Jupiter. He saw that the moon was not flat, as people commonly believed, but that it had high and low areas, and he even calculated the height of some of its mountains. He perceived the Milky Way as a vast collection of stars, and by studying sunspots he reached the conclusion that the sun rotates. *Thus with his telescope Galileo was able to make some important contributions to astronomy.*

Sometimes the topic sentence is not stated at all but is implied. No single sentence in this paragraph states the topic, but it can be implied as "The Renaissance produced many creative men":

Among the great men of the Renaissance, many were artists, like Raphael, Titian, Michelangelo, Van Dyke, and

Rembrandt. Others were poets, such as Spenser, Shakespeare, Tasso, and Ronsard. Still others were pioneers in science: Galileo and Kepler in astronomy, for instance, and Vesalius and Harvey in medicine.

Development

Adequate substance consists of definite ideas, impressions, and observations. Generalizations are frequently trite, vague, and ineffective. Note the lack of substance in this paragraph:

Cheating never pays. After all, "honesty is the best policy"; also when one gets something for nothing he does not appreciate it. I think that every student should be on his own, even if his "own" is not good enough for him to pass his courses. One should be honest, no matter what the cost. The student who thinks cheating is a sin only when it is detected is fooling nobody but himself. Sooner or later, his sins will find him out, and he will have nobody but himself to blame.

This paragraph is more effective when it contains a specific illustration:

Cheating never pays. A friend of mine, whom we shall call John, thought that it did. He once said to me: "Why should I study when it is so easy to get the desired results without work? The only sin in cheating is being caught." And so John was dishonest all through his four years at school. But when he took the college board examinations, he could not cheat because the proctors were efficient. He failed and was bitterly disappointed because he wanted very badly to enter ————— College. Now he believes, as I do, that cheating never pays.

In your study of history or science, it may have occurred to you that in the past some daring thinker or some new discovery or invention has been ridiculed. Such shortsightedness and contempt now seem savage and unbelievable, just as men of the twenty-first century may regard some of our oversights and intolerances as incredible. Not long ago, a writer seized upon the idea that some great thinkers and innovators have been laughed at or scorned by their contemporaries. He did some reading and jotted down some of his findings about these subjects: de Forest, the locomotive, the automobile, Daguerre, the vacuum tube, Murdoch, coal gas, and Socrates. These notes, combined with some hard thinking and rewriting, enabled him to produce this paragraph filled with solid, informative, arresting substance:

> History follows a disturbing pattern of denouncing great discoveries, only to honor them after the discoverers themselves are destroyed or ridiculed by their detractors. For centuries, men have honored the teachings of Socrates as preserved in the *Dialogues* of Plato, but the man himself was condemned to death for corrupting youth with his novel ideas. Lee de Forest was prosecuted for using the mails to defraud because he wrote that his vacuum tube "would transmit the human voice across the Atlantic." And this was as recent as 1913! Daguerre, the creator of photography, was committed to an insane asylum for insisting that he could transfer a likeness to a tin plate. The automobile was opposed because agriculture was felt to be doomed by a vehicle that ate neither oats nor hay. Stephenson's locomotive was denounced on the grounds that its speed would shatter men's minds and bodies. The eminent Sir Walter Scott called William Murdoch a madman for proposing to light the streets of London with coal gas, and the great Emperor Napoleon laughed off the idea as a "crazy notion." Some churchmen argued against the plan as being blasphemous, since God had divided the light from darkness. And some physicians insisted coal-gas lights would induce people to stay out late and catch cold. Who are the heretics and madmen of the 1970's who will be honored and acclaimed a decade or century from now?

Various methods of developing topic sentences involve using different kinds of material in different ways. All methods of paragraph development have essentially the same purpose, however, and the different technical names to label material are of little importance. The primary aim in writing paragraphs is to make the reader see exactly and fully the ideas contained in the expressed or implied topic sentences. The only test of the substance of a paragraph is that of communication. *Define* if the terms are not clear; *explain in detail* if the idea is difficult or abstruse; *give instances and examples* that will relate to the reader's experience and understanding; *compare* or *contrast* the idea with something the reader already knows.

Experienced writers do not say to themselves: "Now I shall give an illustration and example to develop the thought of this paragraph." Many writers would find it almost impossible to define and explain the kinds of substance they use. Nevertheless, a good writer does put flesh on the bare bones of a topic sentence. He asks himself, "What could I do to get across my idea more clearly?" Then his mind sorts through all the available examples and evidence to weed out the most convincing and effective.

The following paragraphs are developed fully and interestingly. Each is "fleshed out" by a different method. Careful study of them will provide suggestions for developing your own paragraphs.

Instances or examples

It is important to remember that, in the strict sense, there is no such thing as an uneducated man. Take an extreme case. Suppose that an adult man, in the full vigor of his faculties, could be suddenly placed in the world, as Adam is said to have been, and then left to do as he best might. How long would he be left uneducated? Not five minutes. Nature would begin to teach him, through the eye, the ear, the touch, the properties of objects. Pain and pleasure would be at his elbow, telling him to do this and avoid that; and by slow degrees the man would receive an education which, if narrow, would be thorough, real, and adequate to his circumstances, though there would be no extras and very few accomplishments.

—Thomas Henry Huxley

Comparison and contrast

The oblique band of sunlight which followed her through the door became the young wife well. It illuminated her as her presence illuminated the heath. *In her movements, in her gaze, she reminded the beholder of the feathered creatures who lived around her home.* All similes and allegories concerning her began and ended with birds. There was as much variety in her motions as in their flight. When she was musing, she was a kestrel, which hangs in the air by an invisible motion of its wings. When she was in a high wind, her light body was blown against trees and banks like a heron's. When she was frightened, she darted noiselessly like a kingfisher. When she was serene, she skimmed like a swallow, and that is how she was moving now.

—From *The Return of the Native*, by Thomas Hardy

Division

The question—*"Which is the happiest season of life?"*— being referred to an aged man, he replied: "When spring comes, and in the soft air the buds are breaking on the trees, and they are covered with blossoms, I think, 'How beautiful is Spring!' And when the summer comes, and covers the trees with its heavy foliage, and singing birds are among the branches, I think, 'How beautiful is Summer!' When autumn loads them with golden fruit, and their leaves bear the gorgeous tint of frost, I think, 'How beautiful is Autumn!' And when it is sere winter, and there is neither foliage nor fruit, then I look up through the leafless branches, as I never could until now, and see the stars shine."

—Author unknown

Combination of methods

The following paragraph possesses elements of contrast, example, and descriptive details:

Nature is a genuine artist. The skill of an artist is estimable, but no one can ever be the artist that Nature is. Nature has the advantage of possessing skill and originality, whereas people can do little but copy the works of Nature. The four seasons of the year provide a variety of subjects for the artist to work with: the fresh bright greens of the grass, buds, and leaves in spring, the lavish multi-varied colors of flowers in summer, the gorgeous red, yellow, and brown leaves of the autumn season, and the delicate lacework etchings of frost on window panes in winter. These are all among the subject-models which Nature gives the human artist to choose from. When such an artist attempts to duplicate the colors and designs of Nature's subjects, he finds it impossible to duplicate them exactly. True, he may come close, but some slight or even major difference is always evident.

Proportion and length

The lengths and proportions of paragraphs in a piece of writing should be determined by the writer's purpose and by the importance of paragraph ideas. However much an idea appeals to the writer, dwelling at length upon it may distort its significance for the reader. Here are five suggestions for proportioning paragraphs:

1. View the subject as a whole before writing.
2. Allot a tentative number of words for the development of each paragraph, but be ready to change this allotment when necessary.
3. Determine the central purpose of each paragraph in communicating ideas to your reader.
4. Lengthen a paragraph if its central idea seems to need amplification, illustration, definition, or any other sort of material that will make clear to your reader what is in your mind.
5. Shorten a paragraph if it does not possess enough significance, even though the words in it appeal to you.

Paragraph length, like paragraph proportion, should be regulated by a writer's purpose and the significance of its ideas. No specific rule is valid, except this one: Do not thoughtlessly or artificially avoid either long or short paragraphs, but keep away from series of either. A successive group of short paragraphs will soon become monotonous and will create an impression of sketchy, inadequate development. Long paragraphs all too often contain unrelated material and thus violate the principle of paragraph unity, the problem to be discussed in Step Fifteen.

STEP FIFTEEN

Make Paragraphs Unified

As each of us knows only too well, our minds do not always work logically. We may think of an idea, possibly a significant one, that should appear in what we are writing but that does not bear upon the subject immediately at hand. If it is included where it does not belong, a reader who is prepared for a discussion of topic A will be confused by a remark concerning topic B.

Notice how the italicized sentence in the following paragraph switches the subject. It is a good sentence and may well belong somewhere in the article but not in this particular paragraph:

> Lake-of-the-Woods is an excellent place for the sportsman to spend the summer. If you like to fish, there are all kinds of fresh-water fish to be found, the most common of which is the pike. A few miles away, up in the mountains, the streams are filled with brook trout. *For people who like to winter-fish, there is ice-fishing nearly every day.* People who are fishing there for the first time can obtain guides, leaving the town early in the morning before the weather gets hot and returning in the cool of the evening.

Again, notice the disrupting effect that the italicized sentence has upon the central thought of this paragraph:

> Our government is primarily one of lawyers and bureaucrats who seem to feel that any attempt to root out gobbledygook is an attack upon their own livelihood. The present

tax law, a creation of lawyers, is gleefully enforced by bureaucrats. *The Social Security Act was passed in 1935 and has had several major amendments since then.* Since nobody, including lawyers, knows exactly what our tax code means, lawyers can enjoy never-ending litigation.

With this principle of unity in mind, try to pick out the sentences in each of the following paragraphs that should not appear:

There are many superstitions all over the world. In some foreign countries like New Guinea, superstitions have more meaning to the people than they do here in the United States. Many people believe in superstitions to the extent that they would stake their lives on them. However, the other group of people disbelieve in superstitions. I am one of these people who disbelieve them, and I am proceeding to tell why I do.

Thanksgiving is always a happy time at my home. This is the time of year to be thankful for all the things we have in this country. Thanksgiving was first started by the Pilgrims during the time of the foundation of our country. The Pilgrims left England in September, 1620, and arrived at Plymouth in November. They had a long, hard winter; many died. But the following year was prosperous, and in gratitude to God they celebrated the first Thanksgiving with prayers and a bountiful feast. They invited many Indians to the feast. At Thanksgiving our family is always together for at least one time during the year. Sometimes we have friends in for dinner; at other times we have a large family reunion. When all of the relatives are present, everyone has a wonderful time.

Any idea that is not related to the main thought of the paragraph should be omitted or placed in another paragraph where it does belong. The only test for unity is this: Does the statement refer to the thought contained in the expressed or implied topic sentence? Let each paragraph develop and convey its own idea— and no other.

Spell It Right

Misspelling is not the most serious error a writer can commit. Having nothing much to say and no purpose and interest in saying it are far more damaging. Nevertheless, correct spelling is essential for intelligent communication. Furthermore, some of your friends and all your employers, business associates, and possible editors will think of misspellings as major mistakes.

Spelling English words is often difficult. For centuries, many words have been spelled "without rime or reason." Through this lack of sensible method, the spelling of many words has become fixed. Many words which sound alike are spelled differently; many words are not spelled as they sound; many contain silent letters. Also, spelling by analogy or common sense is far from a safe guide.

The first and most important step in correct spelling is to have the desire to learn, really to want to become a competent speller. The second is to devote the necessary time to learn. The third is to use all available means to learn.

Remember these words of an experienced teacher of spelling: "All investigations indicate that any *child* of normal intelligence can learn to spell with very little difficulty in a reasonable length of time." Other spelling authorities assert that the common causes of poor spelling are *carelessness* and *laziness*.

Most people are not, by birth and constitution, chronic misspellers, but many do have trouble with spelling. In addition to desire, time, and means, it is well to use a little practical thinking and come to realize that spelling correctly is not an impossible problem.

Perhaps you are one of those people who feel disturbed by their spelling errors and have enough of a spelling conscience to do something about it. Or perhaps you are among those who doubt their ability to master this difficult subject. You may have tried many times and failed. If so, is there any hope for you?

The answer is that if you really have a desire to learn to spell perfectly you can, provided:

1. You can pronounce such words as *accept* and *except* so that they will not sound exactly alike.
2. You can look at such words as *sad* and *sand* and in a single glance, without moving your eyes, detect the difference between them.
3. You can sign your name without looking at the paper on which you are writing and without even consciously thinking about what you are doing.
4. You can tell your friend Bill from your friend Sam by a mere glance.
5. You can learn a simple rhyme, such as "Old King Cole was a merry old soul . . ."
6. You can remember that a compl*i*ment is "what *I* like to get."
7. You can learn the alphabet, if you do not know it already.
8. You can equip yourself with a reliable desk dictionary.
9. You can learn what a syllable is and proofread your writing syllable-by-syllable.
10. You have normal intelligence, here defined as the ability to read and write simple English and keep out of the way of speeding automobiles.

If you can honestly meet these ten provisions, you can learn to spell *without ever making a mistake*. If you can pass Number 10 and only three or four of the others, you can still double your spelling efficiency. It's worth trying, isn't it?

There is no *one* best method of learning to spell correctly. What works for you may not work for your friend, and vice versa. But six approaches are effective, one or more of which may work for you. Learning to spell is an individual matter, so that one of these methods is certain to be more helpful than others. Here are the six approaches:

1. Mentally see words as well as hear them.
2. Pronounce words correctly and carefully.
3. Use a dictionary.
4. Learn a few simple rules of spelling.
5. Use memory devices.
6. Spell carefully to avoid errors.

1. Words should be seen as well as heard

The ability to visualize words, to see them in the mind's eye, is the hallmark of the good speller. When a word is mentioned, a proficient speller can "see" the word in full detail, every letter standing out, as though it were written down before him. Here is a method of learning to see words mentally:

1. With your eyes on the word being studied, pronounce it carefully. If you don't know the proper pronunciation, consult a dictionary.
2. Study each individual letter in the word; if the word has more than one syllable, separate the syllables and focus on each one in turn.
3. *Close your eyes* and pronounce and spell the word either letter by letter or syllable by syllable, depending on its length.
4. Look at the word again to make certain that you have recalled it correctly.
5. Practice this alternate fixing of the image and its recall until you are certain that you can instantly "see" the word under any circumstances and at any time.

Such a procedure is especially valuable when dealing with tricky words that add or drop letters for no apparent reason, that contain silent letters, or that transpose or change letters without logical cause: *explain* but *explanation, curious* but *curiosity, proceed* but *procedure, maintain* but *maintenance, pronounce* but *pronunciation, fire* but *fiery.*

The most frequent error in visualizing words is mistaking one word for another to which it bears some resemblance: *accept* and *except*; *adapt* and *adopt*; *affect* and *effect*; *all together* and *altogether*; *beach* and *beech*; *breath* and *breathe*; *council* and *counsel*; *formally* and *formerly*; *its* and *it's*; *loose* and *lose*; *pillar* and *pillow*; *statue, stature,* and *statute*; *want, wont,* and *won't.*

Literally thousands of "look-alikes" and "sound-alikes" such as these suggest that you become visual-minded if you wish to improve your spelling.

2. Pronounce words carefully and correctly

Spelling consciousness, an awareness of words, depends in part on correct pronunciation. Properly pronouncing the following words will help some persons to spell them correctly; mispronouncing them will cause nearly everyone spelling trouble: carton, cartoon; celery, salary; color, collar; concur, conquer; elicit, illicit; finally, finely; minister, minster; pastor, pasture; plaintiff, plaintive; sink, zinc; specie, species; tenet, tenant.

Here are seven specific suggestions to keep in mind:

1. Do not add vowels or consonants in pronouncing such words as *athletics, disastrous, height,* and *similar,* and you will not misspell them as "ath*a*letics or ath*e*letics," "dis-ast*e*rous," "heigh*th*," and "simil*i*ar."
2. Do not omit consonants in pronouncing such words as *environment, February, government,* and *library.*
3. Do not omit syllables in pronouncing *accidentally, criticism, laboratory, miniature, sophomore,* and you will not misspell them as "accidently," "critcism," "labratory" or "labortory," "minature," and "sophmore."
4. Carefully examine words that contain silent letters: *subtle, muscle, pneumonia, psychology, handsome, would, solemn, listen,* and many, many others.
5. Watch the prefixes of words: *perform* and *perhaps* (not *preform* and *prehaps*), *prefix* (not *perfix*), *proposal* (not *porposal*).
6. Beware of words containing lightly stressed syllables:

dollar, grammar, mathematics, professor. Exaggerate the trouble spots: *dollAr, grammAr, mathEmatics, professOr.*

7. Form the habit of pronouncing and spelling troublesome words syllable by syllable, writing them, and then pronouncing them aloud in order to relate the sound to the spelling.

3. Use a dictionary

When you are doubtful about the spelling of any word, you should check it immediately in your dictionary. You should not, however, have to spend half your writing time flipping pages of the dictionary rather than communicating. Intelligent use of a dictionary can help to prevent trouble. That is, certain approaches to the vast amount of knowledge recorded in a dictionary can fix helpful principles and patterns in your mind so that you do not have to consult it for, at most, more than 5 percent of the words you use. Certain facts about word derivations, prefixes, suffixes, plurals, apostrophes, hyphens, and capitalization can be learned easily—facts that apply to large numbers and classes of words and that help to improve your spelling in wholesale fashion.

4. Learn a few simple rules of spelling

If you happen to study carefully a number of words that have similar characteristics, you can make some generalizations about their spelling. In fact, observers have been doing just this for more than a century, with the result that nearly fifty spelling rules have been formulated.

Generalizations about the groupings of letters that form classes of words do help some people to spell more correctly. The five basic rules given below are of particular value in spelling correctly certain classes of words:

WORDS CONTAINING *ei* OR *ie*

About 1,000 fairly common words contain *ei* or *ie*. It helps to know that *ie* occurs in about twice as many words as *ei*, but the problem is not thereby fully solved. The basic rule may be stated in this well-known verse:

> Write *i* before *e*
> Except after *c*
> Or when sounded like *a*
> As in *neighbor* and *weigh*.

This rule, or principle, applies only when the pronunciation of *ie* or *ei* is a long *e* (as in *he*) or the sound of the *a* in *pale*.

Here is another way to summarize the rule and its reverse: When the sound is long *e* (as in *piece*) put *i* before *e* except after *c*. When the sound is not long *e* (as it is not in *weigh*) put *e* before *i*.

Still another way to state the principle is this: When the *e* sound is long, *e* comes first after *c*, but *i* comes first after all other consonants: ceiling, conceit, conceive, deceit, perceive, receipt, receive, achieve, aggrieve, cashier, chandelier, handkerchief, hygiene, reprieve, retrieve.

This much of the rule is fairly simple. The last two lines of the verse refer to words in which *ei* sounds like *a*. Fortunately, only a few everyday words, such as the following, fall in this group: chow mein, eight, feint, freight, heinous, neighbor, reign, veil, vein, weight.

A few words are exceptions to this basic *ei-ie* rule or are not fully covered by the verse. The best advice is to learn the following words by some method other than trying to apply the rule, which doesn't work: either, Fahrenheit, fiery, financier, height, leisure, neither, protein, seize, sleight, stein, weird.

FINAL *e*

Hundreds of everyday words end in *e*, and thousands more consist of such words plus suffixes: *care, careful, hope, hopeful*. In our pronunciation nearly all *e*'s at the ends of words are silent: *advice, give, live*. Actually the usual function of a final silent *e* is to make the syllable long: *rate* but *rat, mete* but *met, bite* but *bit, note* but *not*.

Final silent *e* is usually dropped before a suffix beginning with a vowel but is usually retained before a suffix beginning with a consonant.

advise, advising	ice, icy
amuse, amusing, amusement	like, likable
argue, arguing	love, lovable
arrive, arrival	move, movable
bare, barely, bareness	owe, owing
believe, believable	purchase, purchasing
care, careful, careless	safe, safety
come, coming	sincere, sincerely
desire, desirable	use, usable, useless
dine, dining	value, valuable
excite, exciting	whole, wholesome
extreme, extremely	

This basic rule is clear enough, but it does not cover all words ending in silent *e*. Here are additions and exceptions to the general principle.

Silent *e* is retained when *ing* is added to certain words, largely to prevent them from being confused with other words.

> *dye, dyeing*, to contrast with *die, dying*
> *singe, singeing*, to contrast with *sing, singing*
> *tinge, tingeing*, to contrast with *ting, tinging*

Silent *e* is retained in still other words before a suffix beginning with a vowel. Sometimes this is done for the sake of pronunciation, sometimes for no logical reason at all: *acre, acreage*; *cage, cagey*; *courage, courageous*; *here, herein*; *mile, mileage*; *service, serviceable*; *shoe, shoeing*.

FINAL *y*

Words ending in *y* preceded by a consonant usually change *y* to *i* before any suffix except one beginning with *i*: angry, angrily; beauty, beautiful; carry, carries, carrying; dignify, dignified, dignifying; happy, happier, happiness; lucky, luckier, luckily; marry, married, marriage; pity, pitiful, pitying.

Words ending in *y* preceded by a vowel do not change *y* to *i* before suffixes or other endings: annoy, annoyed, annoyance; betray, betrayal, betraying; buy, buyer, buying.

Here are some everyday words that follow neither part or the "final y" principle: baby, babyhood; busy, busyness; day, daily; lay, laid; shy, shyly, shyness.

DOUBLING FINAL CONSONANT

Most words of one syllable and words of more than one that are accented on the last syllable, when ending in a single consonant (except x) preceded by a single vowel, double the consonant before adding an ending beginning with a vowel. This is a complicated rule but a helpful one, as may be seen: *run, running*; *plan, planning*; *forget, forgettable*. Several important exceptions, however, should be noted: *transfer, transferable*; *gas, gases*. Note, also, that the rule applies only to words accented on the last syllable: *refer, referred*, but *reference*; *prefer, preferred*, but *preference*.

"ONE-PLUS-ONE" RULE

When a prefix ends in the same letter with which the main part of the word begins, be sure that both letters are included. When the main part of a word ends in the same consonant with which a suffix begins, be sure that both consonants are included. When two words are combined, the first ending with the same letter with which the second begins, be sure that both letters are included. Here are some examples: accidentally, bathhouse, bookkeeping, cruelly, dissatisfied, irresponsible, misspelling, overrated, really, roommate, suddenness, unnecessary.

The only important exception to this rule is *eighteen*, which, of course, is not spelled "eightteen." Also, keep in mind that three of the same consonant are never written solidly together: *cross-stitch*, not "crossstitch"; *still life* or *still-life*, not "stilllife."

5. Use memory devices

One kind of memory device has the rather imposing name of *mnemonics*. The word is pronounced "ne-MON-iks" and comes from a Greek word meaning "to remember." A *mnemonic* is a special aid to memory, a memory "trick" based on what psychologists refer to as "association of ideas," remembering something by associating it with something else. You have been using mnemonics most of your life.

A mnemonic will be most helpful when you base it upon some happening or some person in your life. That is, you must invent, or use, only mnemonics that have a *personal* association of ideas.

Here are a few examples of mnemonics. They may not help you because they have no personal association, but they will provide ideas for the manufacture of your own:

> *all right*: Two words. Associate with *all correct* or *all wrong*.
> *argument*: I lost an *e* in that *argument*.
> *business*: *Business* is no *sin*.
> *compliment*: A comp*l*iment is what *I* like to get.
> *corps*: Don't kill a live body of men with an *e* (corpse).
> *dessert*: Strawberry sundae (double *s*).
> *piece*: Have a *piece* of *pie*.
> *potatoes*: *Potatoes* have eyes and *toes*.
> *together*: TO - get - her.
> *vaccine*: Vaccine is measured in cubic centimeters (*cc*'s).

6. Spell carefully to avoid errors

When writing, you concentrate on what you are trying to say and not on such matters as grammar, punctuation, and spelling. This concentration is both proper and understandable. But in your absorption you are quite likely to make errors of various sorts, including some in spelling, that result from haste or carelessness, not ignorance.

Since many English words really are difficult to spell, we should be careful with those we actually know; yet it is the simple, easy words nearly everyone *can* spell that cause over half the errors made. Listed below are twelve words or phrases repeatedly found misspelled. They are so easy that you are likely to look at them scornfully and say "I would never misspell any one of them." The fact is that you probably do misspell some of these words on occasion, or other words just as simple.

a lot, *not* alot	research, *not* reaserch
all right, *not* alright	religion, *not* regilion
doesn't, *not* does'nt	surprise, *not* supprise
forty, *not* fourty	thoroughly, *not* throughly
high school, *not* highschool	whether, *not* wheather
ninety, *not* ninty	wouldn't, *not* would'nt

Learning to spell is an individual, highly personal matter. One attack on correct spelling will work for one person but not for another. Perhaps it would be more precise to say that although certain words cause trouble for a majority of people, any list of commonly misspelled words will contain some that give you no difficulty and omit others that do. The best list of words for you to study is the one you prepare yourself to meet your own needs and shortcomings.

Once again, correct spelling is less important than many other phases of the writing process. But "spelling it right" is a significant step toward better writing.

STEP SEVENTEEN

Punctuate It Right

When you talk you do not depend upon words alone to tell your listener what you mean. Facial and bodily movements and gestures add much to the words themselves: you shrug a shoulder, wiggle a finger, raise an eyebrow, wink, clasp hands, bend forward or backward, grin or grimace, stamp your foot, nod or shake your head. The tone, stress, and pitch of your voice influence the meanings of words you speak: you yell or whisper; speak calmly or angrily; lower or raise your voice at the end of a statement or a question. Meaning in talk is affected by pauses and halts which can be as significant as words themselves. Nearly everyone has seen a skilled actor convey ideas and moods without using words at all.

Similarly, when we write we cannot expect words alone to make clear to our reader what we have (or think we have) in mind. The pauses, stresses, and inflections that occur in speech must be represented in writing by various marks of punctuation if meaning is to be fully clear. The needs of the eye are quite different from those of the voice and ear.

Punctuation came into existence solely to help make clear the meaning of written words. Every mark of punctuation is a shorthand device or road sign provided to assist the reader along his way. Punctuation is effective if it helps the reader to understand; it is harmful or ineffective if it impedes the flow of thought from writer to reader.

Consider the matter this way: a question mark in writing is

related to the rising inflection in one's voice when he asks a question. The mark indicates to the reader, "You have just read a group of words which should be interpreted as a question." An exclamation point conveys an idea of surprise or determination or command which would be indicated by a strongly emotional tone in speaking. A period represents the pause which occurs in speaking when one idea has been stated and another is perhaps to be expressed; it signals to the reader, "What you have just read is a statement, a sentence or sentence-equivalent." A comma indicates a shorter pause than a period or question mark or exclamation point or, indeed, than several other marks of punctuation.

Proper punctuation is essential to clear, correct, effective writing because it actually helps to express thoughts and the relationships of thoughts.

The most important marks of punctuation are these:

.	Period	,	Comma
?	Question mark	;	Semicolon
!	Exclamation point	:	Colon
—	Dash	" "	Double quotation marks
-	Hyphen	' '	Single quotation marks
'	Apostrophe	( )	Parentheses and [ ] brackets

The most often-used of these marks are discussed in following pages. In addition to marks of punctuation, other devices known as the *mechanics* of writing play a significant but somewhat less important role in writing: italics, capital letters, abbreviations, numbers, and various miscellaneous marks such as the caret and several accent marks. Less-used marks of punctuation, as well as mechanics, are not mentioned as a part of Step Seventeen, but if you are dedicated to the goal of becoming a better writer you should study their uses in a handbook or manual devoted exclusively to the full range of punctuation.

It will help to remember that punctuation serves one of four purposes: to terminate (put a stop to); to introduce; to separate; to enclose.

Termination

Even the most long-winded speaker eventually runs out of breath and must end a statement in order to inhale and start again. In writing, as in speech, the basic unit of thought is the sentence. Now, a sentence, in speech or in writing, may vary in length from one word to many hundreds, but it has to end somewhere, some time. When you come to the end of a statement in speech, you are likely to lower (drop) your voice and to pause before proceeding. In writing, the end of a statement is always correctly noted by an end-stop (terminal mark of punctuation).

The period is used to end nine out of ten sentences. However, if your statement is in the form of a question, you use a question mark to end it. Or if the statement expresses surprise, strong emotion, or a command of some sort, it may properly be terminated by an exclamation point. The use of these three terminal marks will have a distinct influence upon the meaning conveyed:

> What do you mean? You are leaving this town.
> What? Do you mean you are leaving this town?
> What! Do you mean you are leaving this town?

Other marks of punctuation are occasionally used to terminate a statement. A colon may be used to end what is actually an introductory statement when that which follows begins with a capital letter. A statement which is broken off or interrupted may be ended with a dash. Also, a statement left unfinished may be terminated by ellipsis periods (three dots). Four dots may be used at the end of a sentence requiring a period; this practice is rarely observed in most contemporary publications.

> This is what he said to me: Start at once and keep going.
> "I hardly know what to say to express—" The speaker halted abruptly.
> Perhaps I should have kept quiet. Perhaps I should have protested. Perhaps . . .

Introduction

In writing as in speech, we often lead up to a statement with a preliminary one or pave the way for a comment with words that serve as an introduction. Only three of the marks of punctuation are regularly used to introduce words or statements: commas, colons, and dashes. (The sentence which you have just read illustrates this principle; what precedes the colon builds to what follows it.)

> I need only one thing, more time.
> Your task is simple: get a job and hold it.
> He has only one passion in life—dancing.

Separation

For writing to be clear, sometimes individual words or groups of words must be separated from others in the same sentence. To separate parts of a sentence, use a comma, a semicolon, a dash, a hyphen, or an apostrophe. Remember, though, that these five marks cannot be used interchangeably for this purpose.

> If you wish me to go, please lend me some money.
> This man loves his work and is happy; that one hates his and is miserable.
> To separate parts of a sentence—use a comma, semicolon, dash, hyphen, or apostrophe.
> He is now our president-elect.
> This store is crowded every day from noon until 2 o'clock.

Enclosure

To enclose parts of a sentence or longer units of expression, use commas, dashes, quotation marks, single quotation marks, parentheses, and brackets. Enclosing marks are always used in pairs (two of each) except when a capital letter at the beginning of a sentence takes the place of one of them or when a terminal mark of punctuation replaces the second.

> An unusual habit, eating two breakfasts every day, seemed to make him sluggish during morning hours.

He was not—and everyone knew this—a well man.

"I am not an American," he said fatuously; "I am a citizen of the world."

"To say this dance is 'peachy' is not a useful comment," remarked the fireman.

When I am ready to go (and that will be soon) I shall let him know.

"The foreman on this job [Ned Stephens] is an excellent worker himself," remarked the superintendent.

Different marks indicating the four principal purposes of punctuation are not always interchangeable. Both the comma and the dash, for example, can introduce, separate, and enclose material, but this ability does not mean that one is not preferable to the other in a given sentence designed to convey a particular meaning. To achieve the specific purpose of punctuation which you have in mind, select the mark which will most effectively transmit the meaning intended.

The foregoing remarks, combined with what you knew previously about punctuation, may be as far as you need or wish to go with Step Seventeen. For readers who wish more detail, information follows about specific uses of the more widely used marks of punctuation.

1. THE PERIOD

1. A complete declarative sentence should be followed by a period.

> We walked hand in hand through the courtyard. The moon had risen early and was now directly overhead.

Do not use a period after a sentence fragment unless it obviously stands for a complete expression.

Right: I want to send a telegram.
        All right.
        When will it reach Chicago?
        By midnight.

Wrong: Eating cake with a lot of icing.
             When the other people saw him.

2. Use a period before a decimal, to separate dollars and cents, and to precede cents written alone.

5.95 (five and ninety-five one-hundredths); $4.98; $.34.

3. Use a period after a mildly imperative sentence, an exclamation point after a strongly imperative sentence.

Don't step on the broken glass.
Stop that noise!

4. Use a period after a standard abbreviation.

Henry Sutter, Ph.D.; Hon. Paul Stevens (b. 1924; d. 1969); Sept. 15; bbl.; etc.; Atlas Fruit Corp.

Periods are not used after such contractions as *I'm, you've, can't,* or after ordinal numbers when written *1st, 2nd, 3rd, 5th,* etc. *Percent* or *per cent* (abbreviation of *per centum*) does not require a period. Do not use a period after a nickname: *Steve, Al, Ed.*

Inside a sentence, the abbreviation period is followed by any logical punctuation which would be used regardless of the period. If an abbreviation concludes a declarative sentence, a single period is used; if the sentence is interrogatory or exclamatory, a question mark or exclamation point follows the abbreviation period.

The boy weighed 150 lbs., but he made a better tackle than players who weighed over 170 lbs.
Have you counted all the pins, buttons, snaps, etc.?

5. Use three ellipsis periods to indicate an intentional omission from a sentence or quotation.

"Uneasy lies the head . . ."
". . . beggars would ride."

At the end of a sentence, some writers use four periods, the first (or last) indicating the period and the other three the ellipsis periods. A question mark, comma, or exclamation point may precede or follow ellipsis periods.

> Who knows what would happen if . . . ?
> "What a piece of work is man . . . !"
> ". . . 'tis a consummation devoutly to be wished. . . ."

2. THE COMMA

The comma has many distinct uses and therefore causes trouble to many writers. Always used within the sentence, it indicates a brief pause rather than a full stop. The comma, semi-colon, and period may be considered a series in degree of strength. The strongest mark, the period, points out the most important division of thought, the sentence; the semicolon, less strong, divides longer and more important groups of thought *within* the sentence; the comma, weakest of the three, separates short and closely connected groups of thought within the sentence.

More than any other mark of punctuation, the comma depends for correct usage upon the writer's full understanding of precisely what he wants to say.

1. Use a comma to separate independent clauses joined by the coordinating conjunctions *but, and, yet, or, for, neither, nor.*

> Her heart was pounding, for the envelope bore the ancient Crowell crest.
> He knocked on the door, but all sounds within the house had ceased.

When clauses are short—generally speaking, when they consist of only subject and verb—the comma may be omitted.

> John laughed and I cried.
> He stumbled but he never stopped.

Avoid omitting a comma when the result may be momentary confusion.

> We cut the *ribbon and the mayor* spoke. (Supply a comma after *ribbon.*)

When the connection between long clauses is particularly close, the comma is sometimes omitted. Again, if the subject of two separated verbs is the same, the comma is often left out.

Nearly everybody in the country likes ice cream and so it may be called our national dessert.

Some people eat it every day and care nothing about counting calories.

2. Use a comma to set off an introductory dependent clause.

Because I could not swim, I was afraid to go sailing.

Although he tried, he could not dance on roller skates.

If dancing on roller skates was her idea of entertainment, she was welcome to it.

3. Use commas to separate a series of words, phrases, or clauses.

Matilda tossed out her duffel, climbed down the ladder, and eloped with Arnold.

They hopped, skipped, and jumped in the meadow.

However, if serial clauses themselves contain commas, they should be separated by semicolons:

I purchased an old, cracked mirror; a twisted, rusty bicycle wheel which could be gilded; and a new, frightfully gaudy, candy-striped lampshade.

4. Use commas to separate words, phrases, or clauses which are parenthetical.

His marks, *truth to tell*, were not impressive.

However, another bus is on the way.

Shoes, *although she wore them*, felt extremely uncomfortable.

Sentence elements deliberately inserted for forcefulness are somewhat like parenthetical words, and they should be enclosed by commas. Such expressions are emphatic, suspended, or transposed.

She was a pretty girl, a real beauty, and she captivated him. (Emphatic)

His jogging pace was uneven, not only because his knee hurt severely, but because his left sneaker had picked up a wad of chewing gum. (Suspended)

His business was taken over, lock and stock and barrel, by a new management team. (Transposed)

5. Use commas to separate *nonrestrictive* phrases and clauses from the remainder of the sentence.

Phrases and clauses which do not serve to identify the word they modify should be enclosed by commas; those which are essential to the meaning of the sentence should not be enclosed.

This car, *which has power steering*, is for sale. (Nonrestrictive)

The car *that is equipped with power steering* is for sale. (Restrictive)

In the first sentence, *which has power steering* is incidental information and its omission does not materially affect the meaning. It is therefore nonrestrictive and is set off by commas. In the second sentence, *that is equipped with power steering* is essential to the identification of the car in question. It is restrictive and is not, therefore, set off.

The stranger, *cold and weary*, was given lodging for the night. (Nonrestrictive)

The man *warming his hands at the fire* is a stranger. (Restrictive)

Occasionally the *context* in which the phrase or clause appears will determine whether it is restrictive or nonrestrictive.

The man *who ordered champagne* was a violinist.

We were intrigued by the man sitting next to us in the restaurant. His impeccably tailored suit covered a thickset frame, but the rings he wore drew attention to hands of incredible delicacy. The man, *who ordered champagne*, was a violinist.

In the first sentence, *who ordered champagne* is restrictive. But in the second example, the main point is the man's occupation and not the fact that he ordered champagne. Thus, *who ordered champagne* is nonrestrictive.

6. Use commas to set off absolute phrases.

An absolute phrase is one which has no syntactical relation to any word in the sentence.

The food having disappeared, bears were no longer interested in the campsite.

He plunged into the water, *a knife in his teeth*, and came up under the shark.

7. Commas should separate dates, initials or titles, and places. Because such items are really parenthetical, a pair of commas is required.

He worked in Banff, Alberta, until August 30, 1966, when he left Canada for a job in California.

Daniel Reilly, M.D., and Charles Horwitt, D.D.S., occupy this suite of offices.

8. Vocatives, words used in direct address, should be set off.

Bear in mind, *my lad*, that money does not grow on trees.

Cuthbert, I did it all for you!

9. Words in apposition should be separated by commas.

Markham, *a Tasmanian*, owned a pimiento farm.

The assignment, *to dance with every man in the room*, we accepted enthusiastically.

Sometimes the appositive is restrictive or part of a proper name, in which case omit the comma.

The legendary jewel thief *Raffles* is my idea of a charming rogue.

10. Use a comma to set off a short quotation from the remainder of the sentence.

Sweeney inquired, "Is a Rolls Royce a good car?"
"He is not to be believed," she said.

Genuine quotations, however, should be distinguished from quoted material which forms the subject or object of a verb. The latter should not be separated from the remainder of the sentence.

"Don't give up the ship" is useless advice after you've hit an iceberg.
Marie Antoinette little imagined what effect her words would have when she retorted "Let them eat cake."

11. Use a comma to prevent misreading.

Inside the house was painted blue. (Supply a comma after *inside*.)
What I want to know is is it legitimate? (Supply a comma after the first *is*.)
Beyond the ocean could be heard, like rolling drums. (Supply a comma after *beyond*.)

Constructions which can be misread are usually faulty. If possible, rephrase the sentence to remove the awkwardness.
12. Do not use unnecessary commas.
Commas should be used only when they are essential to the sense of a construction. Fewer commas are used in modern writing than was formerly the practice. Be particularly careful not to separate closely related sentence elements. Do not separate a subject and its verb or a verb and its complement: noun phrases act as subjects and objects and should be treated accordingly.

Incorrect: The waitress asked, if we wanted dessert.
             The cap hanging next to the umbrella, is my son's.
             He answered promptly, that he will expect me tomorrow.

Do not carelessly use a comma to replace a word you have omitted.

Incorrect: She said, she was going to the dance. (The comma is incorrectly substituted for the word *that*.)

Unless you intend to stress the idea implied by a conjunction, do not use a comma after the conjunction.

Incorrect: But, James could spell the word correctly.

Do not use a comma before the first or after the last item in a series:

Incorrect: We are going to visit, Rome, Florence, Milan, and Venice.
He owns a fast, expensive, automobile.

3. THE SEMICOLON

The semicolon is a more emphatic mark of punctuation than the comma, signifying a longer pause or break between sentence elements. It is not, of course, as forceful a separation as a terminal mark (period, question mark, or exclamation point). Its uses are clearly established and easily understood. Entirely a mark of coordination, the semicolon is used only between elements of equal rank.

1. Use the semicolon to separate coordinate clauses *not* joined by a conjunction.

She will enjoy the movie; she has always liked melodrama.
Set another place at the table; I'm bringing a guest home for dinner.

2. Use the semicolon to separate coordinate clauses joined by a conjunction if the clauses are lengthy or contain internal punctuation. Also, use semicolons to separate long phrases, clauses, and series of words in which extreme clearness is necessary.

She made sure that the beds were made, the rugs were vacuumed, and the furniture was dusted; and then she felt that she was prepared for her mother-in-law's visit.

3. Use the semicolon to separate coordinate clauses joined by a conjunctive adverb (*therefore, still, also, then, however, thus, so,* etc.)

> Philbrick had lived in Chicago for many years; *consequently*, his knowledge of the city was considerable.
>
> I overcooked the roast lamb; *still*, you may eat it if you wish.

Be sure to distinguish a conjunctive adverb, which has an adverbial function, from a simple subordinating conjunction such as *because, whereas, inasmuch as.* Conjunctive adverbs are used only between independent clauses.

4. THE COLON

The colon is used primarily as a mark for introducing lists, series, quotations, and explanations.

1. Use the colon after an introductory statement which indicates that something is to follow, such as a list, tabulation, or explanation.

> Every religion centers about one overriding principle: man's love for his fellow man.
>
> Everything was in good shape: the house painted, the lawn mowed, the hedge trimmed.

Overuse of the colon should be avoided. In such a sentence as "The three most popular water sports are: swimming, sailing, and fishing," the colon is unjustified and should be omitted.

2. Use the colon to separate introductory words from a quotation which follows, if the quotation is long, separately paragraphed, or formal.

> Stephen Spender has written: "Most people live in a stupor of contentment alternating with a stupor of discontentment."
>
> The conductor then replied: "I would rather perform Beethoven's Fifth Symphony adequately than perform a miraculous operation, be the first man to orbit another planet, or build a magnificent cathedral."

3. A colon is used after the formal salutation in a letter.

Gentlemen:
Dear Mr. Jones:
Dear Sir:

4. A colon may be used to separate hour and minute figures in writing time, the act from the scene of a play, the title of a book from the subtitle.

9:15
Othello III:2
The Practical Navigator: A Handbook of Piloting

5. THE QUESTION MARK

1. Use a question mark at the end of every direct question.

What time is it?
Is this the way to South Kent?

Do not, however, use a question mark when the question is indirect.

Wrong: I asked the cook if we were having fish for dinner?
Right: I asked the cook if we were having fish for dinner.

2. A question mark, in parentheses, is occasionally used to express doubt or uncertainty.

She demonstrated a brand-new (?) dance step.

6. THE EXCLAMATION POINT

1. Use the exclamation point to express emphasis, surprise, command, or other forceful emotion.

Help!
Stop that!

Use the exclamation point sparingly, to express genuine and strong feeling; overuse of this mark weakens its effectiveness.

2. An exclamation point, often enclosed in parentheses, may be used to indicate irony.

He told me he worshipped (!) my cooking.

7. THE APOSTROPHE

1. Use an apostrophe and *s* to form the possessive of a noun not ending in *s*.

Boy's, cat's, driver's, teacher's.
By the day's end his sister's elbow had stopped hurting.

Never use an apostrophe with the possessive pronouns *its*, *theirs*, *yours*, *hers*, etc.

2. Use an apostrophe alone to form the possessive of a plural noun ending in *s*.

Dogs', heads', cousins', students'.

3. Use the apostrophe alone, or the apostrophe with *s*, to form the possessive of singular nouns ending in *s*.

Yeats', or Yeats's (not Yeat's).
Jones', or Jones's (not Jone's).

If the addition of the apostrophe and *s* makes pronouncing the word difficult, add only the apostrophe.

Sophocles', Xerxes'.

4. Use an apostrophe to show that figures or letters have been omitted.

The winter of '68, o'clock, can't, didn't.
There *isn't* a day this week *that's* not filled with appointments.

5. Use an apostrophe when indicating plurals of letters, figures, or words.

How many *s*'s appear in the word *Mississippi*?
You use too many *why's* and *how's* to suit me.

Never confuse the contraction *it's* and the possessive *its*.

> *It's* never too late to learn punctuation.
> Virtue is *its* own reward.

6. When indicating joint or group possession, add an apostrophe and *s* to the last member. Similarly, add an apostrophe and *s* to the last member of a compound word.

> I particularly like *Cross and Blackwell's* marmalade.
> I will use *nobody else's* pocket comb.

7. Do not use an apostrophe unnecessarily.

> The Johnson's came to visit.

An apostrophe is not required; *Johnsons* is simply the plural of the name.

8. QUOTATION MARKS

1. Use quotation marks to enclose every direct quotation.

> She asked, "Did that essay really take you a month to write?"
> "Indeed it did," he replied. "I had to do a lot of research."

If a direct quotation extends to several paragraphs, place quotation marks at the beginning of each paragraph but at the end of only the last paragraph.

2. Use quotation marks to indicate provincialisms and technical words employed in general writing.

> He "sashayed" over to the drugstore.
> He gunned the motor and "laid a strip," as the downshifters say.
> Their delay was caused by a "stack-up" over the airport.

3. Use single quotation marks to indicate a quotation within a quotation.

The singer said: "When I told him he was half a beat be-hind me, he answered, 'Mind your own business,' and threw the music at me."

In dialogue, every change of speaker should have a separate paragraph.

"We can't get a present for Mother," Bob said sadly.
"Haven't we enough money?" asked Sue.
"Sure, but she wants us to forget her age."
"Well, we'll remember the occasion and forget the count."

4. Place quotation marks correctly in relation to other punctuation. The comma and the period are placed *inside* quotation marks.

"Don't go sledding today," she begged. "It's too cold."

Unless it is a part of the quotation itself, place every question mark, exclamation point, and dash *outside* the quotation marks.

Did she say, "My heart's in the highlands"?
He asked, "What are you thinking?"
What is meant by "tarred and feathered"?
She said, "I'm leaving now"—but I wouldn't allow it.
This one's a "lulu"!
"It's a 'lulu'!" he exclaimed.

Semicolons and colons are placed *outside* the quotation marks.

Sing "The Battle Hymn of the Republic"; it's my all-time favorite.

Remember that all quotation marks come in pairs, so that the beginning and end of the quotation are made clear.

5. Do not put quotation marks around an indirect quotation.

Wrong: The conductor asked "how many of us planned to get off at Bridgeport."

Right: The conductor asked how many of us planned to
           get off at Bridgeport.
           The conductor asked, "How many of you plan to
           get off at Bridgeport?"

9. PARENTHESES AND BRACKETS

Although both are intended to set off enclosed material,
parentheses and brackets have separate functions. Parentheses
are used by an author to set off his *own words* from his *own
text*. Brackets are used to set off insertions made by someone
other than the author. Editorial comments, explanations, corrections, and similar material should be enclosed in brackets.
Furthermore, all interpolations by an author or editor in *quoted*
material should be placed within brackets.

1. Use parentheses to enclose parenthetical material which is
remotely connected with the context.

   This omelet (perhaps the eggs were not fresh) has very
little taste.
   Around 509 B.C. (the date cannot be verified) the Republic of Rome was founded.

Because material in parentheses merely amplifies the thought,
some writers prefer to set it off with dashes; indeed, the marks
are interchangeable. When the parenthetical material forms a
complete sentence, the general practice is to use parentheses.

2. Use parentheses to enclose figures which are repeated to
insure accuracy.

   Please send me twenty-six (26) boxes of your miniature
ball-point pens.
   The hotel manager charged them fifty-seven dollars
($57.00) for the week's lodging.

3. Use parentheses to enclose references and directions.

   Northwestern colleges (see pp. 48-58) offer many opportunities to go mountain climbing.

4. Use brackets to enclose a comment of the writer interpolated in a quoted passage.

"I do not find it [the proposed office building] suitable to my purposes," he announced.

10. THE HYPHEN

More a mark of spelling than of punctuation, the hyphen indicates two words or two parts of one word which belong together. It is a unifying device in forming compound words and a mark of division when words must be broken at the end of a line.

1. Use a hyphen to join the parts of a compound word.

Rules for forming compound words are many, various, and sometimes inconsistent. In general, however, hyphens are used:

Between two or more words intended as a single adjective: *blue-eyed*, a *hit-and-run* accident; in *one-two-three* order; his *get-up-and-go* enthusiasm.

Between the numerator and denominator of a fraction: a *two-thirds* majority.

Between the parts of compound numerals in the range of twenty-one through ninety-nine: *seventy-two*; *thirty-six*.

Between the parts of certain compound verbs, adverbs, and nouns: to *freeze-dry* a food; a *well-nigh* perfect performance; *writer-director*.

2. Use a hyphen to mark the division of a word broken at the end of a line.

I shall arrange to meet him at the airport whenever his plane is scheduled to land.

The hyphen should be placed at the *end* of the first line, never at the beginning of the second.

Words of one syllable cannot be divided and must be written whole: *came, though, look, search, school, bright.*

There are various rules for dividing words; however, consulting a dictionary for correct syllabication of given words is a more direct means to proper use of the hyphen in division than attempting to master and apply those rules. Even so, the following suggestions may be used as simple guides:

Two consonants may usually be divided: *mar-/ginal*; *cran-/berry*.

Prefixes and suffixes may be separated: *un-/usual*; *co-/ordinate*; *port-/able*.

Compound words are divided between their main parts: *further-/more*, not *fur-/thermore*.

In addition to the major functions set forth above, the hyphen has a few minor uses:

To indicate the spelling of a word: *Notice that r-o-u-g-h and c-o-u-g-h are pronounced quite differently.*

To suggest stuttering or hesitation in speech: "M-m-may I c-c-carry your books, S-s-sue?"

To represent a dialectal pronunciation: "He came back a-sighin' and a-moanin' for the girl he left behind."

To designate certain street addresses and consecutive numbers: *His office is located at Suite 203-16 Medical Arts Building. The fair will be held December 8-15.*

To codify certain telephone numbers: *215-337-5487*; or account numbers: *RX-1009-86-22501.*

11. THE DASH

The dash is a useful and dramatic mark of punctuation, but it should not be used too often or indiscriminately. Careless substitution of a dash for a period, a semicolon, or colon results in a choppy, incoherent style. When typing, use two hyphens to make a dash.

1. Use the dash to set off sharply distinguished parenthetical material, for emphasis or suspense.

Everyone in this room—there will be no exception—must submit to a lie-detector test.

He will always—always, I assure you—regret that he turned down the job.

2. Use the dash to indicate a shifting or breaking of thought.

We'll solve it this way—but you're not listening.
I wanted to tell you—oh well, it isn't important.

3. Use the dash to indicate the omission of words or letters.

Theodore R—was one of the conspirators.
Look at pages 10-16 of this magazine.

STEP EIGHTEEN

Revise Everything You Write

In everything anyone writes errors of one sort or another are inevitable. Not even a skilled professional writer can preplan, write, and proofread all at one time. Especially not skilled writers—they know from long experience that first drafts are only the beginning of the writing process.

In commenting on the rewriting that went into his famed novel, *The Sound and the Fury*, William Faulkner said simply, "I wrote it five separate times." Truman Capote, author of many works of fiction and nonfiction including *In Cold Blood*, said of all his work; "I write my first version in pencil. Then I do a complete revision, also in longhand. I think of myself as a stylist, and stylists can become notoriously obsessed with the placing of a comma, the weight of a semicolon. Obsessions of this sort, and the time I take over them, irritate me beyond endurance."

Want more proof? Thornton Wilder, the eminent dramatist and novelist, once said, "My wastepaper basket is filled with works that went a quarter through. . . . I forget which of the great sonneteers said 'One line in the fourteen comes from the ceiling, the others have to be adjusted around it.' There are passages in every novel whose first writing is the last. But it's the joint and cement between those passages that take a great deal of rewriting. . . . Each sentence is a skeleton accompanied by enormous activity of rejection."

When asked about rewriting, the short story writer Frank

O'Connor replied that he did so "endlessly, endlessly, endlessly." Then he added, "And I keep on rewriting after something is published."

Alberto Moravia, a widely respected and popular writer, commented: "Each book is worked over several times. I like to compare my method with that of painters centuries ago, proceeding from layer to layer. The first draft is quite crude, by no means finished. After that, I rewrite it many times— apply as many layers—as I feel to be necessary."

Are you still unconvinced that all writing, even that of craftsmen, requires revision? Then listen to this from James Thurber when asked "Is the act of writing easy for you?" His response: "It's mostly a question of rewriting. It's part of a constant attempt to make the finished version smooth, to make it seem effortless. A story I've been working on was rewritten fifteen complete times. There must have been 240,000 words in all. I must have spent 2,000 hours working on it. Yet the finished version is only 20,000 words." And when asked "Then it's rare that your work comes out right the first time?" Mr. Thurber replied, "Well, my wife took a look at a first version and said 'That's high school stuff.' I had to tell her to wait until the seventh draft."

Such comments make writing seem like hard work. Well, it is. But actually there is no such thing as good writing. There is only good rewriting. Those unwilling to revise and rewrite are skipping a major step toward becoming better writers. You may not wish to go to the lengths mentioned here, but some revision and rewriting are essential steps toward making any composition of whatever kind more effective and appealing.

Three kinds of alteration are possible in revision. You can (1) *substitute*, (2) *delete*, and (3) *add*.

In substituting, you can shift from one word to another that seems more accurate or meaningful. You can change the structure of a sentence. You might notice that all the sentences in a given paragraph are about the same length and, to avoid monotony, decide to combine a couple of them. If an example you have given does not seem to make your point, you can substitute another. Many other methods of substitution are possible and readily available, but these hints will give you the idea.

Similarly with deletions: words, sentences, and entire paragraphs can be dropped when they are thought not to pull their weight, fail to make the desired point, or are just plain wordy. In fact, omission is often the most significant and telling of all exercises in revision.

In rereading something you have written, it may occur to you that something more is needed: another fact, another example, an incident or anecdote. For example, Robert Louis Stevenson, in his essay "An Apology for Idlers," wrote this sentence "The services of no single individual are indispensable." The sentence is clear in meaning and well phrased. But isn't it possible that, when revising his essay, the author said to himself "Something is lacking"? Perhaps so, perhaps not. Anyway, Stevenson followed with this memorable sentence, "Atlas was just a gentleman with a protracted nightmare." The idea is now unmistakable and unforgettable. Just as hindsight is always superior to present sight, so "second thoughts" are often better than first ones.

Possibly the process of revising will be clearer to you if it is suggested that with everything you write you

1. Check and recheck your choice of words.
2. Consider revising the word order of certain sentences.
3. Alter some figures of speech.
4. Add a bit of dialogue, if suitable.
5. Supply an incident or anecdote to reinforce an idea.
6. Remove any section that seems stale or dull.
7. Examine, and possibly alter, the order of paragraphs.

Yet another approach to rewriting is to ask of anything you write these searching questions:

1. Does my piece of writing have a definite *central purpose* (that is, have I carefully analyzed the topic)?
2. Does my paper have *ample material*?
3. Is this material (substance) *arranged* in a clear, orderly, and logical way?

4. Is this paper *unified*?
5. Is it *clear* in all its parts?
6. Is the material presented so interestingly that it will *appeal* to its readers?
7. Is my writing *correct* in grammatical and mechanical details?

If it occurs to you that these suggestions for rewriting involve largely mechanical matters, then remember that communication is the dominant aim of all writing and that whatever blocks or slows down communication requires removal. It is for this reason that one revises and rewrites in order to remove errors that distort or bury meaning.

But something remains to be done in the rewriting process. That something is to employ whatever devices of style you can so as to smooth and speed your message to the minds of readers.

Scores of devices can help us communicate. The most important elements contributing to effective and pleasing style can be classified under four headings: simplicity, conversational quality, individuality, and concreteness. Other characteristics could be listed, but even these four goals involve refinements of style that can take a lifetime to perfect.

SIMPLICITY

Simplicity does not mean "writing down" to the reader and underestimating either his intelligence or his knowledge. It does mean expressing one's ideas in terms that are clear, logical, and specifically geared to the level (age, education, and so on) of the persons for whom one is writing.

If a subject is so technical that technical terms cannot be avoided, use them—but define them without employing a tone or method insulting to the reader's intelligence. The level of your reading audience will determine how many such terms should be defined and in what detail.

If you have a choice between a long and a short word, use whichever is clearer and more exact—usually, but not always, the short word. Short words are more often clear and sharp, like signs chiseled in the face of a rock; in much writing, and especially in speaking, they are crisp and filled with zest, saying what they "mean" and leaving as little doubt as possible in the mind of reader or hearer. But whether we use long or short words, diction should be as simple and clear as we can make it so that our ideas will move smoothly.

You hear and read many words previously unknown to you. Impressed, you may attempt what hundreds of thousands of others have done: to employ such expressions in speaking and writing not so much for their actual value as to show others how smart you are, how "educated" you are becoming. Enlarging one's vocabulary and using new words purposefully are both worthwhile activities—but they lose meaning when they are pursued for reasons of vanity, self-esteem, or "culture climbing."

No truer statement about simplicity in style exists than this: "A book has one leg on immortality's trophy when the words are for children but the meanings are for men." Simplicity without substance is childish; but great thoughts, like great inventions of whatever kind, achieve much of their effectiveness and power through simplicity. Can you think of any great work of literature, of any great scientific discovery, that is unnecessarily and arbitrarily complex and involved? A good literary selection or an important scientific discovery may be beyond our understanding, but each probably is as simple as it can be and still be what it is.

Over and over, say to yourself "kiss"—*keep it simple, stupid.*

CONVERSATIONAL QUALITY

More than most of us realize, the *conversational* quality of what we read adds an appeal that helps us to grasp the ideas being presented. Conversation is not necessarily informal and relaxed, but good conversation is never so elevated in tone that one feels condescended to. Have you noticed that some writing by eighteenth- and nineteenth-century authors, even ones considered great and timeless, seems formal and pontifical? That writings of more recent vintage are often more relaxed, less didactic and "preachy"?

This difference in attitude toward both subject and reader is partly a matter of diction and sentence structure, but even more a result of later authors descending from their pedestals. Such a statement does not imply that only recent works have a conversational quality and thus are enjoyable to read. Nor does it mean that a good writer, of whatever era, will figuratively remove his jacket and necktie. It does imply that most effective writers have tried not to sound stuffy and ponderous, that without losing their dignity they have labored to infuse a human, friendly quality into their writing. Conversational quality means ease of expression, not sloppy thought; consideration for the reader as one "thinking with" the author and not as a person both ignorant and stupid.

John R. Tunis, one of the more popular and esteemed professional writers of recent years, has said that he tries to write an essay or magazine article as though he were conversing with a dinner companion. By this, he explained, he meant that he tries to use words and expressions that are not dull and stuffy, that he anticipates and answers in his writing the questions his companion would actually raise in conversation, that he provides illustrations and examples designed to keep the attention of his listener and make him or her actually *see* what he is attempting to communicate.

An even greater writer of an earlier time, Laurence Sterne, wrote in *Tristram Shandy*: "Writing, when properly managed [and, being Sterne, he put in parens] (as you may be sure I think mine is) is but another name for conversation."

INDIVIDUALITY

Related to the device of conversational tone is *individuality*, which is often a virtue and, occasionally, a vice in writing. Individuality implies "subjectivity"; when a writer is subjective he is inward-centered and applies his own standards and judgments. A highly subjective writer tends to ignore the needs and appeals of his readers and thinks exclusively of himself, his thoughts, his needs, his aspirations. Such a tendency—the direct opposite of the stylistic quality inherent in conversation—is a definite flaw.

On the other hand, the individuality growing from subjectivity can help in developing a writing style that is effectively communicative. When we read nonfiction such as essays and articles, we want and need to get the author's opinions, not merely a statement of facts, principles, and statistics. We may be dozing through a dull lecture, a flat recital of facts, but we tend to come awake when the lecturer begins to recount a personal experience, to give an eyewitness account, to express his opinions—in short, when he becomes a human being and stops being an automaton or robot.

No reader wishes to be confronted with material that possesses no spark of the writer's individuality, his personality, his subjective processes of thought and reasoning. Nothing is more dull and hence less communicative than writing that "goes through the motions" of setting down borrowed or plagiarized facts with no obvious stamp of the author's mind and personality. Even a research paper, one based on sources other than the writer's thought and experience, will communicate effectively only when it reveals the author's conclusions and judgments.

Prose is seldom wholly objective (unless, of course, it is merely copied from reference sources). However, an excessively subjective composition can be as ineffective as a wholly objective one. If a writer parades his opinions to the exclusion of all other considerations, if his work is studded with "I," if he is not in some respects reader-centered, he commits the error of subjectivity. If his writing is dull, lifeless, static, almost or totally devoid of emotion or personality, he commits the error of objectivity. Both errors are serious, and striking the delicate balance between them is no easy task. But it can be done.

Do such comments about individuality suggest that one must be *original* in his writing style? The answer, both "yes" and "no," depends upon what is meant by "original." No one can reasonably be expected to produce wholly new, entirely fresh ideas and novel ways of conveying them. No one can do this often; perhaps no one now alive can do this *ever*. If he could, he would be as misunderstood as Galileo or Socrates and might lose his job or his life. But originality can and does also mean "independent thought," "individual insight," "constructive imagination." Each of these elements is attainable by nearly everyone. Goethe has wisely summed up this matter of individuality and originality:

> The most original authors of modern times are such not because they create anything new but only because they are able to say things in a manner as if they had never been said before.

You are yourself and no one but yourself. If what you write, or say, reveals in some degree the imprint of your own personality, your particular individuality, then it will have never been said before in quite the same way. It will possess a genuinely important stylistic quality without which it would be dull and spiritless.

CONCRETENESS

Each of us has repeatedly read material that seemingly "made sense" but that left us with only a vague, fuzzy impression of what the author apparently intended us to absorb. Try as we might, we could not come to grips with the author's meaning. We felt we were dealing with cotton, wool, or some such soft and flabby substance that we could not grasp, handle, and move about in our own thought processes. Discouraged or annoyed, we may have decided that the selection had no meaning and no message for us and thus gone on to something else.

One major cause of such a reaction is lack of *concreteness* in writing. The author we were trying unsuccessfully to read may have been using abstract words to express general ideas; he may have forgotten, if indeed he ever knew, that readers' minds respond most readily to the specific, the tangible, the concrete. For example, when we are hungry we don't think of "nutrition" or "nourishment" or even of "food." We think of steak or baked potatoes or chocolate cake.

Actually, we learned everything we know as itemized bits of experience. When we were small, a parent or some other older person pointed out to us a dog, said "See the dog," and ever afterward, a d-o-g had some particular and special meaning for us. Your concept of a "dog" and that of anyone else will differ, but each item of experience in our private store of meanings has a definite, concrete application. In contrast, we feel baffled by abstract words and expressions that have no direct connection with our own backgrounds.

Abstract words are useful in discussing certain ideas and are especially common in such subjects as philosophy and the social sciences, but usually they are less exact, less meaningful, and consequently less effective than concrete words. Because they refer to specific and actual objects or concepts, concrete words have meanings more or less solidly established in the minds of both writer and reader. "Something worn on the human body between shoulders and chin" is rather vague but not entirely abstract. The concept can be made less vague by referring to a *collar* and more concrete by mention of a *ruff*, *shawl collar*, *long point*, *spread collar*, and *button-down*. The word *neckwear* can refer to a "rather long length of soft material such as silk or wool, worn about the neck and usually under a collar." If a speaker or writer uses *necktie*, he is somewhat more specific; if he uses *four-in-hand*, *bow-tie*, or *necktie party*, he is being even more concrete.

Abstract words possess varying degrees of definiteness. Such words as *countryside*, *fear*, and *security* are not particularly specific, but they have more understandable connections with the experiences of most people than terms like *culture*, *duty*, *truth*, and *honor*. The word *carrier*, defined as a means of conveying and transporting, is somewhat abstract but can be made less so by using such terms as *truck*, *car*, *motorcycle*, and *handcar*, or by *mule*, *tank*, *bus*, *half-track*, and *kayak*.

Good writers sometimes use an abstract term because nothing else will fit and then immediately make it more communicative by providing a concrete example of what is meant or by translating its meaning into terms less abstract and vague. Suppose, for example, that you contend that government should intervene as little as possible in our economy and thus you employ the term *laissez-faire*. Is this expression abstract or concrete? An effective writer, Stuart Chase, unwilling to take a chance on his reader's understanding of the term, used it but immediately equated it with a city that had "no traffic system," one where every driver was on his own. Chase then explained *enforced competition* as a system in which "traffic cops protect little cars"; *governmental regulation* as similar to "traffic cops advising drivers how to drive"; *government ownership* as a procedure in which "a traffic officer throws the driver out and gets behind the wheel himself." You may agree or disagree with the writer's definitions and analogies, but at least you know what he means and have been entertained while finding out.

Much of what we remember from our reading of literature—especially of essays, articles, and biography—consists of incidents and anecdotes originally designed by the author to reinforce some abstract concept. The appeal of short stories, plays, novels, and of much poetry lies in the fact that understandable, flesh-and-blood persons are involved in understandable problems and face understandable conflicts. What happens to people, why it happens, and what the results are seem real and exciting to us because happenings are narrated and described in concrete, specific terms that we can grasp as readily as we can observe or face problems and situations in our immediate lives.

Nine-tenths of all good writing consists of being concrete and specific. The other tenth doesn't really matter.

As you take this important step number eighteen, try always to make your writing as simple, conversational, individual, and concrete as you possibly can.

STEP NINETEEN

Proofread Everything You Write

When we read, we see merely the outlines, or shells, of words. Only poor readers need to see individual letters as such; most of us comprehend words and even groups of words at a glance.

But have you ever noticed how much easier it is for you to detect errors in someone else's writing than in your own? This may be because in reading someone else's writing you are *looking* for mistakes. Or it may be that you look more carefully at the writing of someone else than at your own because you are unfamiliar with it and have to focus more sharply in order to comprehend. You already "know" what you are saying.

Whatever the reason for closer scrutiny, in proofreading we narrow the range of our vision and thereby pick up mistakes hitherto unnoticed. In short, we detect careless errors not by reading but by *proofreading*.

Much of the effectiveness of proofreading depends upon the spread of your vision. The following triangle will show you how wide your vision (sight spread) is. Look at the top of the triangle and then down. How far down can you go and still identify each letter in each line at a *single* glance? Your central vision is as wide as the line above the one where you cannot identify each letter *without moving your eyes at all*.

```
                    a
                  a   r
                a   r   d
              a   r   d   c
            a   r   d   c   f
          a   r   d   c   f   g
        a   r   d   c   f   g   x
      a   r   d   c   f   g   x   y
    a   r   d   c   f   g   x   y   z
  a   r   d   c   f   g   x   y   z   p
a   r   d   c   f   g   x   y   z   p   w
```

People differ in their range of vision as they do in nearly everything else. But many people have difficulty in identifying more than six letters at a single glance. Some have a span of vision embracing only three or four letters. Whatever your span, you should not try to exceed it when you are carefully checking for errors. If you do, you are reading—perhaps with excellent understanding—but you are not *proofreading*.

Only proofreading will enable you to eliminate errors caused not by ignorance or stupidity but by carelessness.

Until your writing is set in type, the kind of reading which has just been discussed is actually "manuscript" reading. When your work appears in type it becomes "proof," a term referring to a trial impression from a printing surface taken for inspection and correction. When you read such an impression, you are actually proofreading. To this end, you may wish to become familiar with what is known as "proofreaders' marks," a sample of which follows:

PROOFREADERS' MARKS

OPERATIONAL SIGNS

ℬ	Delete
◡	Close up; delete space
ℬ	Delete and close up
#	Insert space
eq #	Make space between words equal; make leading between lines equal
hr #	Insert hair space
ls	Letterspace
¶	Begin new paragraph
no ¶	Run paragraphs together
□	Move type one em from left or right
⊐	Move right
⊏	Move left
⊐⊏	Center
⊓	Move up
⊔	Move down
=	Straighten type; align horizontally
‖	Align vertically
tr	Transpose
(sp)	Spell out
stet	Let it stand
⤓	Push down type

TYPOGRAPHICAL SIGNS

lc	Lowercase capital letter
cap	Capitalize lowercase letter
sc	Set in small capitals
ital	Set in italic type
rom	Set in roman type
bf	Set in boldface type
wf	Wrong font; set in correct type
X	Reset broken letter
⊘	Reverse (type upside down)

PUNCTUATION MARKS

⌃	Insert comma
⌄	Insert apostrophe (or single quotation mark)
⌄⌄	Insert quotation marks
⊙	Insert period
?	Insert question mark
;	Insert semicolon
:	Insert colon
=	Insert hyphen
M	Insert em dash
N	Insert en dash

From *A Manual of Style*, 12th edition revised, The University of Chicago Press, 1969.

Whether you are reading manuscript or proof, careful, close attention is obligatory for all writers who wish their work to be as error-free as fallible minds, sight, and hands can make it.

Pay Attention to Manuscript Form

What you have to say and the way you say that something are the most important considerations in writing. But neatness, legibility, and orderly method are also important. Try to give your written work the outward form that will guarantee ready communication and a hopefully favorable response from readers.

Suggestions about manuscript form are obviously controlled by what is being written. For example, comments about the kind of paper to use or the need for typing will not usually apply to the writing of personal letters. Office forms usually dictate much about the presentation of memos and activity reports. If you are preparing material for a college class, it is likely that the paper to be used will be prescribed as will be the method of handling margins, writing or typing, and other considerations.

No matter what you are writing, however, you are urged to take sufficient time to ensure that the finished product will not appear sloppy, slovenly, and hastily prepared. Haven't you, for instance, ever been offended by the appearance of a letter received? Didn't it seem to cry out "Here, take this. I owe you a letter but what can I say in the limited time I have? I know it's messy and thin and maybe not even readable, but it's the best I can do right now." A letter that is hard to understand has a difficult time communicating anything but irritation to the recipient. The same is true of many other forms of writing.

Step Twenty, however, assumes that you are preparing material for submission to a publisher of some kind. It assumes therefore that your manuscript—whether a five-line poem or a book-length novel—will be read, handled, and processed by editors, copy editors, typesetters, and proofreaders. It will undergo shipments (mailings) from you to publisher, to printer, and back to you. It should be clean and legible for the convenience of readers; it should be durable to withstand much handling. The suggestions that follow are based upon these necessities.

Paper

Use a good quality of white bond paper of uniform size, preferably 8½ by 11 inches. Before using it, test to make certain that it will survive ink eradicator and will hold corrections in ink. A glazed or transparent stock is hard to work with and is usually not durable enough to withstand much handling.

Typing

All manuscripts should be typewritten on one side of the sheet in double spacing. Use a black, noneradicable ribbon and renew it when it begins to fade into illegibility. (Remember that every manuscript will eventually become smudged and that after repeated handlings faint typing will become unreadable.) Most publishers will refuse to accept mimeographed, photostatic, or ditto copy because it tends to become illegible and is difficult for the copy editor to correct in ink. If such copy is single-spaced, not enough room is left for markings by editors and printers.

Margins

Leave a margin of about 1½ inches at the top and left of each page of your manuscript and of an inch or so at the bottom and right. Try to keep the width of typed lines and the number of lines on a page as uniform as possible throughout a manuscript. (Doing so will help the publisher and printer to estimate quickly and easily the size of the book or length of the article, or whatever, that is to result.)

Numbering

All pages in a manuscript should be numbered from first page to last. Numbers should be placed in the upper right corner of each page, clearly separated from the text. If preferred, the first page can be noted with a numeral placed at the bottom center. Make certain that pages are in proper order.

Corrections

It is a rare manuscript which does not require some final correction, usually consisting of minor changes. (If corrections are extensive, an entire page, or pages, should be retyped.) Last-minute changes are acceptable to a publisher, provided the author shows care and consideration for those who must read—not decipher—the alterations.

An added or altered word or phrase may be written in ink or typed directly above the manuscript line where it is to be inserted. A caret may be used to indicate the point of insertion. Words, sentences, and even whole paragraphs may be deleted by a firm, clear line drawn through them. The following types of corrections are neither recommended nor acceptable to most publishers: (1) typing inserts on slips attached to pages; (2) typing or writing on the reverse of pages; (3) writing in the margins of pages; (4) writing illegibly; (5) using a pencil.

Typescript

Most publishers will not accept manuscripts written by hand. Typescript is more legible than handwriting and, with rare exceptions, is far neater. Also, most experienced writers have found that errors in typescript are more easily detected and corrected than those in handwriting. If you do not know how to type, learning might be a wise investment of time and money.

The physical appearance of a manuscript will attest not only to a writer's typing skill (or lack of it) but to the extent of his concern about the grace and accuracy of his finished work. The appearance of a manuscript is of immense importance in the entire printing and publishing process. A carefully prepared manuscript may well influence the publisher in the author's favor. And if the manuscript is accepted for publication, its appearance will help or hinder the work of editors, designers, estimators, typesetters, and proofreaders. Poorly prepared copy causes delays, added costs, and frayed nerves.

INDEX

Index

One-plus-one rule, 100
Opinion and fact distinguished, 22
Order of words, 60-65
Originality, 9

Paper, 138
Paragraphs, development of, 82-90; instances and examples in, 87; length of, 89-90; methods of developing, 86-89; proportion of, 89-90; topic sentences in, 83-85; unity of, 91-92
Parentheses, 120-121
Period, uses of, 107-109
Plurals, use of apostrophe with, 117-118
Poetic words, 28-29
Post hoc, ergo propter hoc thinking, 21-22
Predication, reducing of, 79-80
Premises in thinking, 20
Preplanning, 6-11
Prewriting, 9-11
Pronouns, shift in use of, 71-72
Pronunciation of words, 96-97
Proofreading, 134-136; marks for use in, 136
Proportion in paragraphs, 89-90
Punctuation, 103-123; marks of, 104; purposes of, 104-107
Purpose in writing, 12-15

Question-begging in thinking, 23
Question marks, 116
Quotation marks, 118-120
Quotations, punctuation of, 112-113

Rambling sentence, 73-74
Reasonable statements, 17-18
Reducing predication, 79-80
Repetition, useless, 80-81
Restrictive phrases and clauses, 111-112

Revision in writing, 124-133
Robinson, James Harvey, quoted, 16
Rules for spelling, 97-100

Schopenhauer, Arthur, quoted, 19
Self-evaluation, 7
Semicolon, 114-115
Sentences, 51-81; complete, 51-55; concise, 76-81; fused, 58-59; grammar and, 51-52; incomplete, 53-55; logical, 66-69; punctuation of, 56-59, 103-123; spliced, 56-58; structure of, 70-72; unity in, 73-75; word order in, 60-65
Separating punctuation, 106
Shifting word meanings, 23
Sight spread, 134-135
Simenon, Georges, quoted, 11
Simplicity in writing, 127-128
Slang, 35-36
Slanting meanings, 23
Specific and general words, 40-41
Speech, origin of, 1
Spelling, 93-102; methods of learning, 95; pronunciation as aid in, 96-97; rules for, 97-100
Split constructions, 64-65; infinitives, 64
Statement of intent, 13
Sterne, Laurence, quoted, 129
Stevenson, Robert Louis, quoted, 126
Style in writing, 127-133
Subject, consistency in, 71
Subjectivity, error of, 19
Suppressed evidence, 22
Syllogism, 20

Tense, consistency in, 70
Terminal punctuation, 105
Testimonials, 25